ENGAGING TEACHERS IN

CLASSROOM

WALKTHROUGHS

ASCD MEMBER BOOK

Many ASCD members received this book as a
member benefit upon its initial release.

Learn more at: **www.ascd.org/memberbooks**

ENGAGING TEACHERS IN
CLASSROOM
WALKTHROUGHS

DONALD S. KACHUR | JUDITH A. STOUT | CLAUDIA L. EDWARDS

ASCD

Alexandria, Virginia USA

1703 N. Beauregard St. • Alexandria, VA 223111714 USA
Phone: 800-933-2723 or 703-578-9600 • Fax: 703-575-5400
Website: www.ascd.org • E-mail: member@ascd.org
Author guidelines: www.ascd.org/write

Gene R. Carter, *Executive Director;* Mary Catherine (MC) Desrosiers, *Chief Program Development Officer;* Richard Papale, *Publisher;* Genny Ostertag, *Acquisitions Editor;* Julie Houtz, *Director, Book Editing & Production;* Jamie Greene, *Editor;* Dayna Elefant, *Senior Graphic Designer;* Mike Kalyan, *Production Manager;* Keith Demmons, *Desktop Publishing Specialist*

All web links in this book are correct as of the publication date below but may have become inactive or otherwise modified since that time. If you notice a deactivated or changed link, please e-mail books@ascd.org with the words "Link Update" in the subject line. In your message, please specify the web link, the book title, and the page number on which the link appears.

ASCD Member Book, No. FY13-8 (July 2013, PSI+). ASCD Member Books mail to Premium (P), Select (S), and Institutional Plus (I+) members on this schedule: Jan., PSI+; Feb., P; Apr., PSI+; May, P; July, PSI+; Aug., P; Sept., PSI+; Nov., PSI+; Dec., P. Select membership was formerly known as Comprehensive membership.

PAPERBACK ISBN: 978-1-4166-1549-1   ASCD product #113024

Also available as an e-book (see Books in Print for the ISBNs).

Quantity discounts: 10–49 copies, 10%; 50+ copies, 15%; for 1,000 or more copies, call 800-933-2723, ext. 5634, or 703-575-5634. For desk copies: www.ascd.org/deskcopy

Library of Congress Cataloging-in-Publication Data

Kachur, Donald S.
  Engaging teachers in classroom walkthroughs / Donald S. Kachur, Judith A. Stout, Claudia L. Edwards.
    pages cm.
  Includes bibliographical references and index.
  ISBN 978-1-4166-1549-1 (pbk. : alk. paper) 1. Observation (Educational method) 2. School improvement programs. I. Stout, Judith A. II. Edwards, Claudia L. III. Title.
  LB1731.6.K34 2013
  371.102--dc23
                         2013008947

22 21 20 19 18 17 16 15 14 13   1 2 3 4 5 6 7 8 9 10 11 12

ENGAGING TEACHERS IN
CLASSROOM
WALKTHROUGHS

Acknowledgments

We express our very deepest gratitude to the educators from various schools and school districts (see Appendix A) for the important contributions they made to our written work. These schools and districts recognize the value of teacher leadership in the classroom walkthrough process. Teachers in these settings were given opportunities to work as partners with administrators in raising the bar on teaching and learning. The educators who worked with us provided detailed descriptions of their classroom walkthroughs, including a wide range of valuable considerations and recommendations. More importantly, they shared the vision, challenges, and successes of teacher participation in a process that provides the very best education for all students.

Many other educators contributed to our stories through conversations and e-mails. They were excited about and supportive of a book that demonstrates the importance of teacher leadership in classroom walkthroughs. Contributors knew firsthand about the benefits of classroom walkthroughs and yet remarked on how little had been written on the subject. We thank them for their encouragement, direction, and reviews of our writing.

The educators we want to acknowledge are

- Marie M. Adair, Executive Director, New Jersey ASCD, Jamesburg, New Jersey
- Mike Almeida, Principal, Alan Shawn Feinstein Middle School, Coventry Public Schools, Coventry, Rhode Island

- Laureen Avery, Director, Northeast Region, UCLA Center X, Los Angeles, California
- Lyn Bair, Principal, Bridges High School, Roaring Fork School District, Carbondale, Colorado
- Paula Bleakley, Principal, Holmes Elementary School, Darien Public Schools, Darien, Connecticut
- Travis Boeh, Associate Principal, Fort Vancouver High School, Vancouver Public Schools, Vancouver, Washington
- Catherine Brown, Academic Intervention Specialist, Cleveland High School, Seattle Public Schools, Seattle, Washington
- Erika Burden, Principal, Westwood Middle School, Cheney Public Schools, Cheney, Washington
- Sarai Carbaugh, Principal, Griffith Elementary School, Sequatchie County Schools, Dunlap, Tennessee
- Jill Carlson, Principal, Crownhill Elementary School, Bremerton School District, Bremerton, Washington
- Lorilyn Caron, Principal, Mohegan Elementary School, Montville Public Schools, Oakdale, Connecticut
- Marsha H. Carr, PreK–5 Supervisor of Special Education, Sequatchie County Schools, Dunlap, Tennessee
- Jaime Castellano, former Superintendent of Schools, Ganado Unified School District, Ganado, Arizona
- Virginia Castro, Principal, E. R. Geddes Elementary School, Baldwin Park Unified School District, Baldwin Park, California
- Maribel Childress, Principal, Monitor Elementary School, Springdale Public Schools, Springdale, Arkansas
- Debra Clemens, Associate Superintendent, Cheney Public Schools, Cheney, Washington
- Eric Conti, Superintendent of Schools, Burlington Public Schools, Burlington, Massachusetts
- Bob Dahm, Program Director and Grants Administrator, Alternative Day School Program, Belleville Township High School District 201, Belleville, Illinois

- Mary Jane Dix, Principal, Leonard J. Tyl Middle School, Montville Public Schools, Oakdale, Connecticut
- Amy Espinoza, Principal, Dr. Charles E. Murphy Elementary School, Montville Public Schools, Oakdale, Connecticut
- Kristen Tepper, Assistant Principal, Eastside High School, Antelope Valley Union High School District, Lancaster, California
- Jaron Fried, Principal, Ball Junior High School, Anaheim Union High School District, Anaheim, California
- Diana Fujimoto, Lesson Design Specialist, Katella High School, Anaheim Union High School District, Anaheim, California
- Andrea Gannon, Director of Curriculum, Belleville Township High School District 201, Belleville, Illinois
- Jennifer Garrison, Superintendent of Schools, Sandoval Community Unit School District 501, Sandoval, Illinois
- Cathy Gassenheimer, Director, Alabama Best Practices Center, Montgomery, Alabama
- Margery Ginsberg, Associate Professor, University of Washington, Seattle, Washington
- Susan Green, Principal, Summit Middle School, Southwest Allen County Schools, Fort Wayne, Indiana
- Bonnie Haffajee, Principal, Randels Elementary School, Carman-Ainsworth Community Schools, Flint, Michigan
- Judy Haptonstall, former Superintendent of Schools, Roaring Fork School District, Glenwood Springs, Colorado
- Ted R. Haynie, Lecturer, Towson University, Towson, Maryland
- Shannon Hoos, Lesson Design Specialist, Ball Junior High School, Anaheim Union High School District, Anaheim, California
- Linda Inglis, Principal, George H. Luck School, Edmonton Public Schools, Edmonton, Alberta, Canada
- Kathryn Kee, Educational Consultant and Leadership Coach, Coaching for Results Global, Hoyt, Kansas
- Sue Kind, BTSA Support Provider/Consulting Teacher, Fontana Unified School District, Fontana, California

- Sue Krapf, Principal, Benton Grade School K–4, Benton School District 47, Benton, Illinois
- Suzanne Lacey, Superintendent of Schools, Talladega County Schools, Talladega, Alabama
- Patrick Larkin, Assistant Superintendent for Learning, Burlington High School, Burlington Public Schools, Burlington, Massachusetts
- Kathy Larson, Education Consultant, Cooperative Education Service Agency #2, Whitewater, Wisconsin
- Sheila Maher, Associate Superintendent for Educational Services, Carrollton–Farmers Branch Independent School District, Carrollton, Texas
- Elba Maisonet, former Principal, Schubert Elementary School, Chicago Public Schools, Chicago, Illinois
- Moriah A. Martin, Assistant to the Associate Superintendent, Office of Human Resources and Development, Montgomery County Public Schools, Rockville, Maryland
- Pat Martinez-Miller, Director of Faculty, UCLA Center X, Los Angeles, California
- Mike Matsuda, Coordinator, Teacher Support and Professional Development, Anaheim Union School District, Anaheim, California
- Brooke Morgan, Assistant Principal, Munford Elementary School, Talladega County School District, Talladega, Alabama
- Kay Musgrove, Executive Director, Tennessee ASCD, Franklin, Tennessee
- Jeff Nelsen, Targeted Leadership Consulting, Los Alamitos, California
- Meuriel Nystrom, Executive Director, Idaho ASCD, Lewiston, Idaho
- Deb Oda, Coordinator of Professional Development, South Junior High School, Anaheim Union High School District, Anaheim, California
- Betty Olson, Principal, South Junior High School, Boise School District, Boise, Idaho
- Karen Olson, Principal, Crystal River Elementary School, Roaring Fork School District, Carbondale, Colorado
- Laurie Pallin, Director of Curriculum and Instruction, Montville Public Schools, Oakdale, Connecticut
- Judy Pearson, Staff Development Teacher, James Hubert Blake High School, Montgomery County Public Schools, Rockville, Maryland

- Howard Pitler, Senior Director for Curriculum and Instruction, Mid-continent Research for Education and Learning, Denver, Colorado
- Stephanie Posey, Principal, Belleville East High School, Belleville Township High School District 201, Belleville, Illinois
- Brooke Puricelli, Principal, DeWitt Perry Middle School, Carrollton–Farmers Branch Independent School District, Carrollton, Texas
- Mike Reed, Principal, Williamsport Area High School, Williamsport Area School District, Williamsport, Pennsylvania
- Pat Roth, Principal, Arroyo Vista Charter School, Chula Vista Elementary School District, Chula Vista, California
- Joshua St. John, Assistant Principal, Summit Middle School, Southwest Allen County Schools, Fort Wayne, Indiana
- Kathleen Schnefke, Literacy Specialist, Parkway Elementary School, Greenwich Public Schools, Greenwich, Connecticut
- Kathy Scott, Principal, Oxford Academy, Anaheim Union High School District, Anaheim, California
- David Shepard, Education Consultant, The Middle Matters, Lexington, Kentucky
- Mike Skelton, Principal, Jonesboro High School, Jonesboro School District, Jonesboro, Arkansas
- Jeff Snell, Deputy Superintendent, Camas School District, Camas, Washington
- David Swierpel, Director of Professional Learning and Community, Carman-Ainsworth Community Schools, Flint, Michigan
- Jeremy Voss, Principal, Basalt Middle School, Roaring Fork School District, Carbondale, Colorado
- Rick Weber, Principal, Huntingtown High School, Calvert County Public Schools, Huntingtown, Maryland
- Alice Wells, Executive Director, Arizona ASCD, Phoenix, Arizona
- Robin Wiltison, Principal, Martin Luther King, Jr. Middle School, Prince George's County Public Schools, Beltsville, Maryland
- Dan Winters, Principal, Salt Creek Elementary School, Chula Vista Elementary School District, Chula Vista, California

Finally, we would be remiss not to recognize ASCD and the all-around support we received in moving this manuscript through a process of reviews, acceptance, editing, revisions, more editing, and final publication preparation. To publish a book goes far beyond just the authors and calls for exceptional teamwork among many talented professionals. In particular, we express our deepest gratitude to Genny Ostertag, Acquisitions Editor, who recognized the potential of this book and encouraged us to submit a manuscript, and to Jamie Greene, Associate Editor, who provided us with continuous and exceptional assistance in shaping this manuscript into a more concise, accurate, and informative portrayal of the subject matter.

Preface

This is a book about classroom walkthroughs. More specifically, this is a book about teacher leadership throughout the classroom walkthrough process. This teacher leadership results in ongoing professional conversations about and growth in improving teaching and learning. Although walkthroughs have historically been regarded as the domain of school administrators, classroom teachers are finally becoming more directly involved in them. Teachers participate in planning, implementing, and evaluating walkthroughs, and they participate as observers and the observed. This is the story we want to tell.

When we first became interested in classroom walkthroughs, we were surprised by how widely this activity was being used as a school improvement tool yet how little the education literature contained on the topic. Initially, we were attracted to nationally known walkthrough models: Data-in-a-Day, Downey's Three-Minute Classroom Walk-Through, Instructional Practices Inventory (IPI) Process, Learning Walk Routine, Look 2 Learning, McREL Power Walkthrough, Instructional Rounds Network, Teachscape *Reflect* Classroom Walkthrough, and the UCLA Center X Classroom Walk-Through. Although they have different purposes and protocols, these models are used by many schools across the country to improve instruction and student learning. We studied these models for several years and gleaned similarities and differences as we presented the topic of classroom walkthroughs at local, state, and national conferences. Those presentations confirmed that many educators were unaware of established walkthrough models or how variations of walkthroughs could serve as school improvement tools.

We realized that once administrators became interested in walkthroughs, they would each seek a model that best fit their unique school setting. We found that many schools across the country had implemented specific walkthrough models but modified them over time to better meet their needs and goals. This observation impressed upon us that, because one model seldom fits all school needs, the best model may be one that is locally modified or designed for implementation. Our original intent was to present readers with an introduction to a wide range of walkthrough models, which would help them acquire a broader sense of how they could be used. That interest became the incentive for our first book, *Classroom Walkthroughs to Improve Teaching and Learning* (Kachur, Stout, & Edwards, 2010). Based on our review and study of various models used across the country, we shared ideas with school leaders that could be drawn from those examples for designing their own walkthrough models.

As we continued to interact with school personnel who were conducting walkthroughs, we found that schools where walkthroughs were sustained and where teaching and learning were improving actively involved their teachers in every aspect of the walkthrough protocol. The trend was shifting away from walkthroughs as something done *to* or *for* teachers to a process undertaken *with* teachers. School administrators were actively partnering with teachers in this educational enterprise. Teachers had an important voice in the design and implementation of the walkthrough protocols and were becoming observers rather than just being observed. These were exciting learning environments in which all staff benefited from opening classrooms for one another to observe, share ideas, discuss issues, and improve individual teaching practices.

Although we were interested in stories about what these schools were doing, we felt that the real stories were about how school leaders (administrators, teacher leaders, and other quasi- or nonadministrative staff) achieved the buy-in from classroom teachers to participate in the walkthrough process and view the visits as valued professional learning experiences. This book highlights the stories and lessons shared by these school leaders. We learned how they overcame the cultural challenges of isolationism and teacher reluctance or resistance to successfully involve their teachers in walkthroughs.

We found school leaders who encouraged teachers to get involved in walkthroughs; teachers leading efforts for change and continuous improvement; and administrators and teachers deciding together to overcome so-called teaching isolationism by promoting greater exchange of teaching ideas. All of these measures contribute to improved student achievement. Some of the schools featured in this book were in their first or second year of actively involving teachers as observers in walkthroughs; others were already five or more years into such involvement.

None of the schools or districts identified in this book claimed that they had "fully arrived" in terms of classroom walkthroughs. Some settings retained pockets of teachers working largely in isolation and spending little time with colleagues to share ideas and address teaching and learning issues. All of these schools and districts are making significant progress, however. Some have achieved a collaborative culture. Teachers regularly participate in the walkthrough process and in subsequent professional conversations. These professional staffs share knowledge about the craft of teaching and explore solutions to challenging learning problems. Most of the schools we studied commented specifically about how their original vision of involving teachers in the walkthrough process changed and evolved as they evaluated the process. This ongoing evaluation of walkthroughs ensured that they met the intended outcomes for which they were designed.

Whether you are a teacher or a school administrator, this book was written for those of you interested in actively engaging classroom teachers in all aspects of walkthroughs. The schools we studied represent a fraction of the many schools that are successfully involving teachers as participants and partners in this process. We hope that your school will have a similar story.

In Chapter 1, "Defining Teacher Leadership in Classroom Walkthroughs," we introduce the concept of walkthroughs as an important school improvement tool. We identify the nature of our work for this book and introduce the schools featured, including the criteria for their selection, how we identified them, and the information we sought from them. We demonstrate the rationale for teacher leadership at the building and district levels, and we share some of the initial questions school leaders are likely to raise when considering involving teachers in classroom walkthroughs.

In Chapter 2, "A School Culture to Support Walkthroughs," we review the features that contribute to a culture in which walkthroughs are accepted, valued, and successful. We share stories from schools explaining the leadership roles of the principal and teachers, the power of shared leadership, the necessity of having an environment of trust and safety, the importance of having a staff that is student-centered, the value of communities of learning, and the role of collaborative inquiry.

In Chapter 3, "Components of Successful Walkthroughs," we discuss the reasons why these schools implemented walkthroughs, the walkthrough models they used, their years of implementation, which teachers do the observing, and the frequency and length of walkthrough observations. We describe the components of teacher walkthroughs, including the focus and looks-fors, methods of recording observation data, and types of follow-up to observations. In particular, we highlight the importance of identifying and implementing steps to affect teaching and learning after teacher walkthrough data have been gathered and shared.

In Chapter 4, "Strategies for Getting Teachers Involved," we summarize the recommendations that schools and districts featured in this book have for those contemplating or actually planning to introduce walkthroughs. These recommendations include involving teacher leaders as advocates for the process; having a clear, definable purpose for the walkthroughs; introducing the process gradually and carefully into the school; ensuring transparency of the entire walkthrough protocol; developing norms to govern walkthrough behaviors; providing walkthrough training; arranging and scheduling walkthroughs and follow-ups; inviting volunteers to begin the process; focusing on students learning rather than teachers teaching; and conducting discussions on walkthrough data without being evaluative or judgmental of teachers.

In Chapter 5, "Additional Issues to Address," we focus on other issues or obstacles that schools may encounter throughout the walkthrough process. Some of these issues are teacher reluctance or resistance, teacher union concerns, coordinating and tracking the walkthrough process, announcing walkthroughs, connecting walkthroughs to other school improvement data and efforts, and evaluating the walkthrough process and measuring the effect it has on teaching and learning.

In Chapter 6, "Concluding Thoughts," we emphasize the value of adjusting walkthrough protocols if the walkthroughs are not meeting expectations. We also highlight the importance of including the Common Core State Standards as a major area of focus for walkthroughs. The meaningful sharing of ideas and experiences through walkthroughs is crucial to building a collective understanding of what the common core should look like in the classroom.

The appendixes include a list of all the schools and school districts featured in this book that have implemented teacher walkthroughs, questions that guided our study of these schools about their walkthrough processes, a sample survey for acquiring teacher input in designing a local walkthrough model, examples of teacher walkthrough observation forms, a step-by-step account of an illustrative walkthrough in practice, and a sample questionnaire for evaluating a classroom walkthrough process.

We hope this book inspires readers, particularly classroom teachers, to collaborate with their professional colleagues and investigate ways to design and implement a classroom walkthrough process that promotes a continuous renewal of teaching and learning in an atmosphere of collegiality and shared mission.

Select figures and the appendixes from this book
can be downloaded at

www.ascd.org/ASCD/pdf/books/walkthroughs2013.pdf

Use the password "ASCD113024" (no quotes)
to unlock the PDF.

CHAPTER 1

Defining Teacher Leadership in Classroom Walkthroughs

Teachers learn best from other teachers in settings where they literally teach each other the art of teaching.

—Judith Warren Little

Classroom walkthroughs have become increasingly popular as a valued tool for the continuous improvement of schools. We interpret classroom walkthroughs as brief, frequent, informal, and focused visits to classrooms by observers for the purposes of gathering data on educational practices and engaging in some type of follow-up. Walkthroughs differ from full-period observations in that they consist of short, quick snapshots. They enable observers to record information over time on features of classrooms including instructional materials and strategies, curriculum standards and lesson objectives, levels of cognitive interaction, student engagement, classroom resources and displays, behavioral management, and more. Walkthroughs differ from most short-term classroom visits in that the observers have a particular focus and set of look-fors in mind as they collect data for subsequent discussion and action.

For the most part, walkthroughs have been used by administrators to better acquaint themselves with the day-to-day operation of a school. However, we know that limiting walkthrough observations to administrators significantly limits the impact of this practice. To obtain all of the benefits of classroom walkthroughs, teachers must be involved throughout the process—from investigating potential implementation to developing the protocol itself to planning for evaluation and revision.

When teachers visit one another's classrooms to gather information on teaching practices and student learning, a wealth of shared knowledge is collected. We are firmly convinced that, in terms of the positions of the people doing classroom observations, the further those people are from the classroom (for example, district-level staff observing classrooms versus teachers observing one another), the less instructional practice will change. In other words, teachers working with their colleagues have the greatest effect on improving teaching practices.

The Rationale for Involving Teachers as Leaders in Walkthroughs

We found a number of important reasons why schools decided to include teachers in walkthroughs. The educators we interviewed were explicit in their belief that classroom observations are a valuable source of professional growth for teachers at every stage of their careers. These educators view walkthroughs as a means for teachers to observe, reflect on, and discuss their practices and to focus on individual, collegial, and schoolwide improvement. They know that the outcome of walkthroughs involving teachers will be greater consistency of instructional best practices across all grade levels and subject areas.

Moriah Martin, former staff development teacher at James Hubert Blake High School, points out that a "principal-only" approach to improving teaching and learning is not effective:

We knew that if teachers did the walkthroughs, they would observe the teaching themselves and could better discuss and identify strong teaching practices. If only principals were doing the observations and then talked about what they saw with the teachers, it would not only be very "top-down," but the school improvement process would not be owned by everyone.

Teachers observing teachers provides opportunities for the teaching staff to (1) note useful practices other than the ones they use; (2) ease the fear of trying something new; (3) feel motivated to improve their craft; (4) identify possible areas for their own professional development; (5) identify areas of practice for reflective dialogue with colleagues; and (6) accelerate improvement in student performance. Walkthroughs are another way for teachers to become responsible for their own professional growth and are an excellent complement to traditional professional development.

The Benefits of Teacher Leadership

Teachers and students directly benefit from teachers collaborating and participating in walkthroughs. Although peer observations can be threatening, when walkthroughs are implemented in a carefully planned, considerate, and respectful manner, the rewards are great. The process will enable members of your school community to engage in dialogue and reflection about teaching practices. Furthermore, we

> We have professional expertise right in our own schools, and we need to take advantage of that, which teacher walkthroughs can help provide.
>
> *—Mike Matsuda,*
> *Coordinator for Quality Teacher Programs,*
> *Anaheim Union High School District*

believe that student achievement is directly linked to collegial collaboration, which is clearly supported by classroom walkthroughs. The whole walkthrough process includes real conversations about teaching, an understanding and use of a common vocabulary, and teachers asking for and providing one another with assistance. Taken together, these benefits have the potential to raise the instructional capacity of a school to a higher level of continuous improvement and performance.

Teachers have traditionally worked in relative isolation, as so-called independent artisans exercising their craft behind closed doors (Bloom, 2007). According to Richard Elmore (2007), privacy of practice produces isolation, and isolation serves as the enemy of improvement. Isolated teachers perceive others as self-reliant, and they are reluctant to ask for help or engage in instructional conversations. They often doubt themselves and believe they are alone in experiencing the challenges and frustrations of teaching. Isolation prevents teachers from disclosing personal strengths, challenges, and needs. By contrast, we promote opportunities for teachers to observe other teachers in action, capturing and sharing the very best practices in teaching and learning. They can work together to support one another's professional growth and development. According to Jeff Nelsen and Amalia Cudeiro (2009),

> Many teachers learn best by observing colleagues using the strategy they are attempting to learn themselves. Having each teacher observe several other teachers practicing a new strategy and discussing what they observed in the initial learning sessions can be a powerful support. It also gives teachers the opportunity to develop a common vocabulary around the new practices and sends a strong message that "We're all in this together." (p. 34)

Compared to other types of professional development, the walkthrough is the most enriching and stimulating. It is an opportunity to see "best" practices in action and debrief and reflect upon those observations with colleagues. What better way to learn? See how something is done, then discuss it to cement an understanding!

—*Mary Lou Bettez,*
7th/8th Grade ELA Teacher,
Alan Shawn Feinstein Middle School

Involving teachers as observers in the walkthrough process can transform the entire school into a learning community and build a culture that values the engagement of teachers in continuous and sustained professional growth. No matter how schools tailor the process, the essentials are the same—teachers learning from teachers in a nonevaluative way, talking about their craft, and developing lessons as a result that will improve student achievement (Blatt, Linsley, & Smith, 2005).

As depicted by the examples in this book, we find that teachers are increasingly buying into the idea that walkthroughs are an effective tool for examining and continuously improving their practice. Teachers take charge of their own learning by collaborating with one another for personal professional development—learning from colleagues through observation, inquiry, dialogue, sharing, and practice. These walkthroughs help staff measure the progress they are making in implementing a new initiative, and they enable teachers to observe effective practices that confirm their own classroom behavior. They can also help teachers acquire new ideas and techniques through one of the most powerful means to learning—watching those ideas and techniques being enacted. Helping teachers feel comfortable with involvement in the walkthrough process is key to making it work for the entire staff as a true professional development and school improvement tool.

Featured Schools

The basis of the work for this book came from our two-year study of 40 schools that were conducting teacher walkthroughs—representing 30 school districts in 17 states and 6 schools from 1 school district in Canada (see Figure 1.1 and Appendix A). The evidence shows that including teachers in the walkthrough process occurs among all types and at all levels of schools. As we studied these schools, our interest was not only in the ways they involved teachers but also in how they created the interest and motivation for teachers to engage in the walkthrough process. We found schools with a variety of approaches to walkthroughs, and we selected schools for our study that

- Implemented a nationally known walkthrough model or designed a brand-new model.
- Were at various stages of implementation of walkthroughs.
- Included different grade levels (elementary, middle, and secondary school).
- Represented neighborhood, charter, and alternative schools.
- Were of various sizes in terms of numbers of teachers and students.
- Included many different populations of students in terms of ethnicity and poverty rates.

- Represented all the geographical regions of the United States.

Our primary means for identifying schools that met these criteria were the following:

- Contacting key individuals from the 18 classroom walkthrough models featured in the book *Classroom Walkthroughs to Improve Teaching and Learning* (Kachur et al., 2010).
- Contacting a network of key educators across the country knowledgeable about schools where peer observations were occurring.
- Contacting executive directors of the ASCD affiliates, who in turn communicated the request to their members.
- Conducting Internet searches on walkthrough models and reports.
- Reviewing the literature on classroom walkthroughs.

In addition to traditional public schools, the study included a Native American school (Ganado Intermediate School), an alternative high school (Bridges High School), and a charter school (Arroyo Vista Charter School). The schools ranged in size from 80 to 2,690 students, with teaching staffs of 6 to 149. The schools represented wide variations of racial and ethnic mixes, and poverty rates ranged from 4 to 99 percent, based on free and reduced lunch program enrollment.

Data Collection

We asked the educators in these schools to share details about their teacher walkthrough processes from inception to evaluation. The educators we contacted included central office personnel, building administrators, and many different kinds of teacher leaders. Our primary purpose was to acquire stories and recommendations we could share with our readers who want to engage their teaching colleagues in the walkthrough process.

The educators with whom we communicated shared their experiences through questionnaires (see Appendix B), phone calls, and e-mails. One round of questions focused on what each school was doing to involve teachers in walkthroughs. The focus of those questions was primarily on the

- Reasons that led to involving teachers in walkthroughs.
- Walkthrough model used.
- Purpose of and participants in the walkthroughs.
- Walkthrough logistics (such as coordination, scheduling, tracking, frequency, and length of visits).
- Selection of the focus and look-fors in walkthroughs.
- Data gathering and follow-up to the observations.
- Roles and responsibilities of the principal in the process.
- Evaluation of the walkthrough process and measure of its effect on teaching and learning.

The second round of questions (see Appendix B) focused on how the schools established walkthroughs that involved teachers and how they addressed

FIGURE 1.1
Location of U.S. Schools in Walkthrough Study

Region	States
Northeast	Connecticut, Massachusetts, Pennsylvania, Rhode Island
Midwest	Illinois, Indiana, Michigan
South	Alabama, Arkansas, Maryland, Tennessee, Texas
West	Arizona, California, Colorado, Idaho, Washington

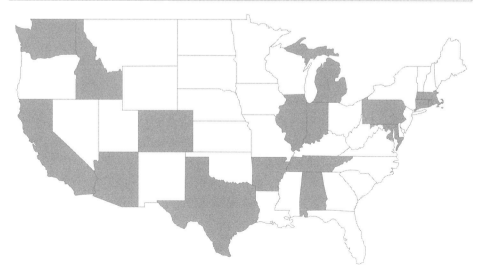

challenges to implementing their walkthrough models. The focus of those questions was primarily on the

- Features of the school culture in place to support teacher leadership in walkthroughs.
- Benefits to the teachers, students, and school.
- Initial steps to implement walkthroughs.
- Connection of the walkthroughs to other school improvement initiatives.
- Issues and obstacles to overcome (such as trust, teachers unions, scheduling, and teacher reluctance or resistance).
- Preparation of teachers for walks (such as training and walking norms).
- Evaluation of the walkthroughs and subsequent effect on teaching and learning.
- Changes to walkthrough purpose, protocols, and practice over time.
- Recommendations for initiating and sustaining walkthroughs.

The information from the surveys and follow-up communications provided us with a rich source of ideas, issues, and recommendations. We believe that sharing what these schools learned will be of great value to those of you who want to involve teachers in the walkthrough process. Such information will contribute to your agenda as you consider the design, implementation, and sustainability of a teacher walkthrough protocol in your school.

Reasons given by schools for involving teachers in the walkthrough process were to

- Share teacher expertise about existing instructional practices and needs.
- Advance the school improvement plan.
- Establish accountability for school initiatives.
- Build team spirit among the teaching staff.
- Determine the progress made in implementing a new initiative after participating in professional development efforts.
- Advance the development of a real professional learning community.
- Track the progress being made in delivering a standards-based learning environment.

District-Driven Emphasis on Classroom Walkthroughs

We found that the initial driving force for some schools implementing walkthroughs was building-level leadership. We also found school districts where central office leadership expected all schools within their jurisdiction to involve their teachers as walkthrough observers. These districts either provided training in a particular walkthrough model for the staff or encouraged and supported individual schools as they explored and implemented their own walkthrough processes. A number of factors contributed to these districts fostering a systemwide teacher walkthrough initiative.

In some cases, districtwide initiatives such as professional learning communities, lesson design specialists, formative assessments, and a student learning protocol were among the catalysts for walkthroughs. A key element for the creation of professional learning communities in Montville Public Schools in Connecticut was to create a culture in every school whereby all staff members learn from one another. Walkthroughs were considered a learning process to enable teachers to identify the instructional areas they wanted to improve and to identify practices to implement in their own classrooms. Anaheim Union High School District in California implemented a districtwide lesson-design initiative that filtered down to each school site. Each school was assigned an instructional design specialist to work with the faculty to develop a collaborative learning community focused on coaching, walkthroughs, and side-by-side lesson design. A districtwide emphasis on the use of formative assessments to

> Every 10 years, our school is involved for three days with an on-site visiting accreditation team. It was frustrating to think that those visiting educators leave our school with a better understanding schoolwide of our instructional practices and needs than our own teachers. Our teachers should be the experts of their own school as to what is taking place and what is needed for school improvement. The walkthroughs are seen as one major vehicle for tapping their expertise.
>
> —*Patrick Larkin, former principal, Burlington High School*

improve student achievement was an incentive for the Talladega County Schools in Alabama to explore walkthroughs that involved teachers. School leaders implemented the Instructional Rounds Network (City, Elmore, Fiarman, & Teitel, 2009), which included cross-functional groups (composed of teachers and administrators or of people in multiple roles) examining formative assessment practices across the entire school district. Individual schools applied the same visitation model at the building level to achieve more immediate and direct impact on school improvement. The Cheney Public Schools in Washington State had a districtwide goal to ensure high-quality teaching and learning in every classroom. A cadre of 80 teachers from across the district was trained in the use of the Student Learning Protocol, a research-based professional development tool that helps teachers focus on instructional practices that make a positive difference on student achievement. Upon completion of the training, each building team of administrators and teachers determined how they could further support and implement walkthroughs using the Student Learning Protocol to inform and strengthen instructional practice.

We do three types of walkthroughs: administrative walkthroughs that involve administrators from other schools and two teacher representatives from the school; teacher-team walkthroughs that involve 11 teachers trained to do the walks; and individual teacher walkthroughs, usually with those teachers visiting colleagues at the same grade level.

—Lorilyn Caron, Principal, Mohegan Elementary School

External funding or state-level education initiatives accelerated interest in walkthroughs in several school districts. Sequatchie County Schools in Tennessee began investigating the use of classroom walkthroughs after the state was awarded Race to the Top funds. Those funds allowed a wide range of professional development opportunities on effective teaching from the Marzano Research Laboratory. That training included instructional rounds in which small groups of teachers make brief observations of their fellow teachers for the primary purpose of comparing and improving their own practice. Work with the Colorado Department of Education in their Closing the Gap pilot provided by Mid-continent Research for Education and Learning (McREL) was the incentive for the Roaring Fork School District to initiate walkthroughs. The district's leaders wanted teachers to invest in the strategies for improved teaching practices presented in *Classroom Instruction That Works* (Dean, Hubbell, Pitler, & Stone, 2012). The walkthroughs were considered a means to establish a common approach among the teaching staffs in delivering high-quality instruction across schools.

Just the awareness of the effectiveness of a particular walkthrough model served as an incentive for several other school districts to invest time and energy into engaging teachers as walkthrough observers. In Burlington School District in Massachusetts, school administrators and department chairs from each of the district's schools initially participated in the Look 2 Learning (L2L) model. Classroom teachers who participated in the training shared what they learned at school staff meetings. As a result of the training, leaders in each school introduced faculty participation into the L2L walkthrough model. Similarly, after attending the Instructional Rounds Institute at Harvard University, school leaders at Carrollton-Farmers Branch School District in Texas created their own model of instructional rounds to support continuous improvement in teaching and learning. Today, the district has five Instructional Rounds networks composed of teachers, support staff, and administrators. Twenty-three host schools and a total of 53 teachers participate in these districtwide visits. Teachers at host schools also participate in internal rounds at the building level, where every teacher is involved to some degree.

A book study in one case and a new-teacher-induction program in another launched districtwide interest in walkthroughs. Staff in Carman-Ainsworth School District in Michigan studied *Classroom Instruction That Works*. The district offered training in the McREL Power Walkthroughs and expanded the pool of those trained to include teacher union leaders and teacher leaders from across the schools. The district leadership wanted to know if the strategies from *Classroom Instruction That Works* were actually being implemented in classrooms. Fontana Unified School District in California requires new teachers to visit classrooms across the district as part of its induction program. The districtwide walkthroughs have a great impact on novices when they visit a wide range of teachers and have time to collaborate with their colleagues about the instructional strategies they observed.

Where to Begin?

Where does a school begin to engage teachers in the practice of classroom walkthroughs? We found that every school had a range of questions at the outset when considering teachers as leaders in the walkthrough process. When Susan Krapf, principal of Benton Grade School K–4 wanted to involve teachers in walkthroughs, she began by asking the following questions:

- Will my staff even want to be involved?
- Do they feel they have the time to add another thing to their plates?
- How do I sell this as a nonthreatening, beneficial learning experience?
- How will we fit this into our day?
- Would my teachers volunteer some of their prep time to participate in walks or cover for another teacher doing walkthroughs?
- Will the district hire substitutes to cover for my teachers conducting walks?
- How often will we do walkthroughs?
- When will teachers meet to talk about walkthrough observations?
- How do I manage to schedule walkthroughs to make them equally accessible to all teachers?
- What will we do with the information gained from the walkthroughs?

Principal Susan Green and her assistant, Joshua St. John, at Summit Middle School had the following questions in mind when they began considering involving teachers as observers:

- What will we do to eliminate potential teacher fear that the purpose of walkthroughs is evaluative?
- Will the walkthroughs be motivating or demotivating to teachers?
- How will we provide time for teachers to conduct walkthroughs and follow-up discussions?
- How will we achieve maximum participation?

- How will we develop a walkthrough documentation form for which all have buy-in?
- What meaningful data (look-fors) should be collected from the walkthroughs?
- Should walkthroughs be announced or unannounced?
- How will we measure the effectiveness of our walkthroughs?

The questions asked by these school leaders represent the questions raised by all schools initially considering the involvement of teachers in walkthroughs. In this book, we share ideas from the participating schools that will guide you in addressing similar questions. Before they will completely buy in to it, teachers must realize the professional value gained from engaging in the walkthrough process.

Success comes from administrators and teachers working together to develop and implement a walkthrough protocol designed to meet a school's improvement goals. We highly recommend that all teachers be involved in the process. Some will be early adopters and some will be more reluctant, but the integrity of the process is maintained when all staff have access to the decision making. We suggest administering a teacher survey such as the one in Appendix C to create a profile of staff views about classroom walkthroughs that you can use in designing your school's model. As with the implementation of any initiative, the process must be regularly evaluated to ensure there is observable improvement in teaching and learning.

Lessons Learned and Moving Forward

Until recently, classroom walkthroughs were an administrator's responsibility. Walkthroughs involving teachers now occur at all levels and types of schools—elementary, junior high/middle, secondary, charter, and alternative. Involving teachers in walkthroughs to observe the dynamics and instruction in other classrooms can have a significant impact on instructional practice. Walkthroughs open doors for educators across the entire school to observe, reflect on, and collaboratively discuss instructional practices and their effect on student learning. Walkthroughs are an excellent alternative or complement to traditional and longstanding forms of professional development, whether they originate as a result of a district initiative or of school leadership planning.

The following chapters offer valuable information about how schools involve teachers in walkthroughs and how to overcome challenges that may arise when making this change to the school's culture.

Questions to Think About

Both teachers and administrators may introduce professional development ideas to the staff at their schools. Questions presented at the end of each chapter are intended to be considered from the point of view of all professional staff. Here are some questions to ponder before launching a walkthrough process involving teachers:

- What districtwide initiatives would be a natural catalyst for the implementation of walkthroughs?
- What benefits of walkthroughs appeal to faculty in your school?
- How can walkthroughs support overall school improvement efforts?
- What opportunities already exist in your school for your teaching colleagues to reflect on and discuss teaching and learning?
- What questions do you have about getting started with walkthroughs?

Our Recommendations

- Examine various models of walkthroughs to select or design a model that meets your school culture, needs, and goals.
- Promote the value of walkthroughs as a means to immediately observe the implementation of new teaching and learning initiatives.
- Link the walkthrough initiative to other school improvement initiatives so they are connected to and supportive of one another.
- Inform prospective teachers during the interviewing and hiring process that walkthroughs are part of your school culture and an important component of your school's professional development.
- Ensure support at the district level for the walkthrough process.

CHAPTER 2

A School Culture to Support Walkthroughs

When professionals share their talents and skills, they help the whole school develop a collective wisdom about learning and teaching.

—Shirley Hord and William Sommers

As we studied schools where teacher leaders were part of the walkthrough process, we were curious about the conditions in place in the school setting that enable this type of peer visitation to be successful. We asked some questions: How committed are teachers to improving teaching and student learning? How committed are teachers to their own continuous learning? What is the level of communication, trust, and collaboration among teachers and between teachers and administrators? How accepting, caring, respecting, and encouraging are teachers of one another? To what extent do teachers feel safe to say what they really think? To what extent are teachers open to examining new ideas and taking risks? To what extent do teachers feel supported rather than judged?

These questions, of course, address components of a school's culture, and the responses to them are subjective in nature. To focus on a school's culture means to look at its deep pattern of values, beliefs, and traditions that have been formed over time. Simply stated, the school's culture can be described as "the way we do things around here" (Deal & Kennedy, 2000). We believe that school cultures can be placed on a continuum from complacent, "satisfied with the status quo" schools on one end to highly cohesive, forward-moving schools on the other. Schools on the complacent end have a great deal of difficulty trying to reestablish their culture so staff members value working and learning together. For such schools, moving forward will cause what Phil Schlechty (2005) refers to as disruptive change because it "calls upon the system and those who work in it to do things they have never done" (p. 3). Well-designed walkthroughs represent a powerful strategy that can help move these schools to a cultural norm of community, collaboration, support, and collective growth.

We asked, "What features of your school's culture needed to be in place for walkthroughs to be accepted and valued?" Respondents identified the importance of the principal's leadership; shared leadership; an environment of trust and safety to encourage risk taking; a student-centered staff; a community of learning in which all faculty are willing to continuously learn by seeking ideas, support, and help from one another; and a commitment to collaborative inquiry. The characteristics, elements, or principles of each of these features contribute significantly to the implementation of effective classroom walk-through protocols. Although we discuss these factors as separate sections in this chapter, they are interdependent in their contribution to school improvement.

School Principal Leadership

The supportive role of the school principal in implementing walkthroughs was strongly reinforced by all of the schools. An effective administrator can champion the process, address teacher concerns, build trust, help schedule time for classroom walkthroughs, give opportunities for all teachers to participate, provide coordination assistance and other resources, and oversee the follow-up to walkthroughs. As the principal at Martin Luther King, Jr. Middle School, clearly affirms, "If the principal doesn't get it, doesn't believe in the importance of the walkthroughs, it will not permeate throughout the teaching staff."

We found many examples of just how important the supportive role of the principal is to successful walkthroughs. In some cases, the principal is out front and actively involved in the process, as demonstrated at Katella High School. Katella's principal was instrumental in laying the groundwork and encouraging teachers to participate as observers. He encouraged those who had participated in walks to persuade others who were not convinced about the value of the experience. This eventually resulted in a shift in Katella's culture whereby teachers are now comfortable having colleagues coming in and out of their classrooms.

The principal at Monitor Elementary School assumed the role of "lead learner" in the classroom walkthrough process. She works with the teaching staff to schedule walkthroughs as a part of the school's master calendar for professional development; helps select the focus for the walkthroughs based on data collected from prior walkthroughs, student achievement data, and professional development initiatives; collaborates with staff to create the over-arching focus question to be explored during each walkthrough and the graphic organizer used for record keeping; and facilitates the reflective conversations following each walkthrough.

The principal at Huntingtown High School assists staff with teacher walkthrough participation; makes sure that all faculty get feedback from the walkthrough observations; arranges time for teachers to meet for reflective discussions; and brings up walkthrough conversations at faculty meetings as input to future school improvement action.

> It is extremely important as principal to be included along with my teachers in the training to conduct a walkthrough process and learn together how best it should work in practice.
>
> *—Bob Dahm, former principal, Belleville West High School*

The principal at South Junior High School in Idaho attends all team meetings, walks with teachers, and helps coordinate the professional development that results from walkthrough data. This principal felt that when she walked regularly with her teachers as a member of the teacher walkthrough team, she continually reinforced the importance of the walkthrough process.

In other cases, we found principals who played a major role behind the scenes, encouraging and supporting their teachers to take responsibility for the walkthrough process. For example, the principal at Crownhill Elementary School removed herself from walkthroughs once the process was in place so that the teachers could "own" it.

After providing walkthrough training for a group of teacher leaders, the principal at Ball Junior High School moved to the sideline. He felt that this shift would help secure buy-in from teachers because they were the ones responsible for the whole process; walkthroughs were not done at his request.

The principals at Belleville East and West High Schools do not participate in follow-up discussions when teachers share walkthrough data and discuss implications for their instructional practices. These principals want to avoid any possibility that their presence would be construed as being evaluative.

These school leaders illustrate the fact that the principal plays a major role in creating and sustaining the culture for successful walkthroughs. A key role of the principal is to involve teacher leaders in the early exploration of walkthroughs to make the implementation more successful.

Shared Leadership

The principal, through shared leadership, involves the staff in creating a vision for walkthroughs as a tool for promoting focused reflective dialogue around teaching and learning. The respondents to our inquiries overwhelmingly indicated that this shared leadership is critical to the success of walkthroughs for the improvement of instruction and learning. Expertise is widely distributed throughout the school rather than being vested in an individual person or position (DuFour, DuFour, & Eaker, 2008). The old model of formal, one-person, top-down leadership leaves the substantial talents of teachers largely untapped (Lambert, 2002).

Shared leadership may involve individual teachers, teacher leaders, or the school leadership team. In some schools, individual teachers or teacher leaders were responsible for promoting interest in walkthroughs among their colleagues. Teacher leaders are typically confident and willing to open their classrooms to visitors. They are not likely to be intimidated by others, are open to learning, and understand the three dimensions of learning in schools: student learning, the learning of colleagues, and their own learning (Lambert, 2003). Because they have the respect of their peers, these teachers play a major role in influencing and promoting a new initiative such as the walkthrough. Teacher leaders are often regarded as key to implementing change and growth in a building. If these informal leaders move forward, then the entire staff will be more likely to support an initiative (Whitaker, 2002). If teacher leaders do not embrace a change, then the chances for success are slim.

Two staff development teacher leaders at James Hubert Blake High School introduced and championed walkthroughs after attending district training. These teacher leaders explained to their colleagues why walkthroughs were beneficial, what could be learned from them, and how the process would be evaluated and adjusted as needed. They made it clear that every teacher would have the opportunity to serve on a walkthrough team. With the leadership of these trusted colleagues, clear guidelines established for the walkthroughs, and plans made for team and whole-group debriefs, the buy-in for walkthroughs was achieved.

A team of educators at Parkway Elementary School was trained in the UCLA Center X Classroom Walk-Through model in the spring of 2006. The team consisted of the principal, the assistant principal, the instructional specialist, a reading specialist, and two classroom teacher leaders. They shared what they learned with the rest of the staff, and this soon led to the implementation of walkthroughs at Parkway. With the support of

We were presented with a walkthrough model early in the year, and some of us volunteered to be a part of the pilot program in our school. After the initial training, we continued to reach out to our colleagues, sending multiple e-mails seeking volunteers for classroom visits. Our curriculum director and building administrators were key in assisting us with coverage for our own classrooms so that we could go on walkthroughs.

—*Sandra Bascetta, Brooke Kleinman, and Erin Dolan, teachers, Leonard J. Tyl Middle School* the administrators, these leaders presented the model to the staff and aroused interest in walkthroughs. Five more teachers attended walkthrough training in the fall. These classroom walkthroughs involving teachers as observers became an important part of Parkway's culture.

The second major personnel group to promote interest in and buy-in from teachers for walkthroughs is the school leadership team (also known by other names, such as building leadership team, school improvement team, site-based management team, learning support team, and organization leadership team). A school leadership team allows more people to contribute to schoolwide decisions.

When teachers have a genuine voice in making professional development decisions, they become more committed to the effort. Under the guidance of the school leadership team, teachers' input on the planning of various dimensions of walkthroughs will lead to their success. This input can help alleviate some of the concerns teachers have with walkthroughs, such as the following:

- The possibility of walkthroughs being used as teacher evaluation.
- A "gotcha" experience of teachers catching their colleagues at a poor teaching moment.
- A misunderstanding about the purpose of the walkthrough.
- Confusion about how the observation data will be used.
- Negative disclosure of a teacher's performance by colleagues to the faculty as a whole.

After field-testing 10 research-validated instructional strategies in the school, the leadership team at Ball Junior High School promoted the introduction of walkthroughs. Early common assessment results demonstrated the effect of identified strategies on improved student performance. The school leadership team members wanted to participate in classroom walkthroughs to observe those strategies across classrooms and provide feedback to the entire staff. Because this was a valuable learning and sharing opportunity, the school leadership team actively recruited fellow teachers to participate in walkthroughs. In one year, the percentage of teachers volunteering to observe rose from 35 percent to 90 percent.

Although the teachers at Katella High School were considered effective, they were used to working in relative isolation. Because of this aspect of the school's culture, school leaders anticipated that many of the 100-plus faculty members would resist the idea of classroom walkthroughs. Members of the school leadership team accepted the challenge and became vocal advocates for the school walkthrough process. Walks began with members of the leadership team and a few other key teachers. This participation established a sense of trust among the staff that the focus of the walks was on what *students* were doing rather than what *teacher*s were doing. Three years later, this high school is now addressing some key schoolwide issues and is able to engage in some difficult conversations because of the trust built as a result of teacher-led classroom walkthroughs.

The new principal at Alan Shawn Feinstein Middle School wanted to initiate the kind of classroom walkthroughs that had been successful at his former school. He and the assistant principal met with the school improvement committee to introduce walkthroughs as one instrumental way of building a professional learning community, collecting data on student learning, and reporting results for reflection and professional development. The effort resulted in the development of literacy walks designed to help teachers self-assess their level of proficiency in formative assessment practices.

Environment of Trust and Safety

We were not surprised to find that *trust* was the very first response given by more than two-thirds of the respondents when they were asked which component of school culture was most necessary for classroom walkthroughs to succeed. Trust is the on-ramp to achieving collaboration and collegiality (Roy, 2007). For many teachers, engaging in walkthroughs means embarking on a new and risky form of professional development—one that "invades" their personal classroom space. Therefore, trust must be developed and sustained among staff members. A huge and growing research base indicates that learning is most effective when it is shared (e.g., Hord & Sommers, 2008). Shared actions based on shared learning are more successful at making long-term, effective changes. Trust is the glue for both of these processes to connect favorably.

> Trust is number one! Trust is important for teachers to feel comfortable opening up their rooms to observation by peers. And it's also number one in getting teachers to participate openly and deeply during reflective conversations following walkthroughs.
>
> —*Maribel Childress,*
> *Principal, Monitor Elementary School*

A lack of trust between teachers and administrators, as well as among teachers, will stymie, if not kill, any new initiative. In walkthroughs, as in other professional development initiatives, teachers must be able to trust the process, their colleagues, and the relationships that ensue. They must also trust themselves in order to fully participate and learn on the job. School improvement becomes an ongoing focus when all staff members take collective responsibility for their own learning and the learning of their students (Hord, 2004). That collective responsibility does not just happen. It must be nurtured by school leadership for it to become part of the culture in schools where student learning is the primary focus and where trust abounds.

An important aspect of building trust is the assurance that this process is nonevaluative. Teachers need to know that the walkthrough process is safe and that they will not be singled out or criticized for their teaching. Some teachers have concerns about whether teachers will report what they observed in their classrooms. Reinforcing the idea that walkthroughs are professional growth opportunities for teacher colleagues can address this fear.

The principal at Crownhill Elementary School mentioned that a school culture of safety ensures that staff members feel comfortable taking risks and talking freely about their learning walks without fearing that the process will be evaluative. Moriah Martin, former staff development teacher at James Hubert Blake High School, emphasizes that teachers must know the walkthrough is safe and that no teachers' names will be used in follow-up discussions:

> Because teacher teams of observers visited so many classrooms in one day, team members were better able to discuss trends in what they saw instead of particular instructional examples of teachers.

Sharing the fact that they would discuss trends and patterns helped to build that safety. In those follow-up discussions, the walkthrough process really focused on overall school improvement, not individual teacher performance.

We believe the evidence of trust in the teacher walkthrough initiative will be demonstrated by (1) sharing leadership with teachers so they are instrumental in the design or selection, implementation, and evaluation of the walkthrough process; (2) supporting teachers with training, resources, and time to work and learn together; and (3) ensuring that communication with and among teachers about the purposes, intentions, and protocols of the walkthroughs is transparent.

> A school that embraces teacher walkthroughs must be a learning community that fosters a climate of trusting and collaborative professionals who are "risk takers" continually striving to improve their practice.
>
> —*Kathleen Schnefke, Literacy Specialist, Parkway Elementary School*

Many of the schools developed norms or guidelines to govern expected behavior of teachers participating in walkthrough observations and subsequent reflective discussions. In most situations, the norms prevented the use of evaluative or judgmental language when recording observations or in debriefing conversations. We discovered that for a number of schools, building a safe environment and reducing risk with teacher walkthroughs were achieved by having teachers scripting exactly what they observed or heard. (We address walkthrough norms in greater detail in Chapter 4.)

Student-Centered Staff

Respondents to our question about culture noted the unremitting focus of their colleagues on students' needs, abilities, experiences, learning styles, and achievement. We learned that student-centered schools are actively involved in developing and advocating shared beliefs, a vision, and actions that promote increased student learning. When a school places the learners and their needs at the center of the equation, it is well positioned for the implementation of walkthroughs. Staff members view performance data as a tool for increasing productivity and are open and willing to ask for professional assistance from colleagues in the interest of increasing student learning.

> Our school culture of concern for our students drives our teacher walkthrough program. Our teachers are open to continuously seeking out and accepting ways to improve our students' learning.
>
> —*Mary Jane Dix, Principal,*
> *Leonard J. Tyl Middle School*

At Belleville East and West High Schools, the staff used their walkthrough process to gather authentic, rich data on student learning that not only propelled student achievement to new levels but also transformed those two high schools into collaborative communities based on student results. The staff at South Junior High School in Idaho value the importance of gathering student learning data from multiple sources. One important source comes from classroom walkthroughs and has led to improvement in teaching that ultimately affects student learning.

In student-centered schools, all staff work together to make sound decisions for continuous school improvement. The data on student learning acquired from both observations of and interactions with students during walkthroughs can complement and corroborate other assessment data on student learning.

Community of Learning

Another important feature of a school culture that embraces walkthroughs is being a community of learning—a place where all participants continue to learn and support the learning of others (Barth, 2002). Members of learning communities know that people learn more readily together than they do on their own. According to Barth (2006), "There is no more powerful way of learning and improving on the job than by observing others and having others observe us" (p. 12). This view is well demonstrated when teachers are observers in the walkthrough process. They can define excellent teaching and classroom practices, share instructional practices and ideologies, and improve individual and overall school performance.

Classroom walkthroughs promote collegiality. Evidence of collegiality is demonstrated when educators (1) talk with one another about their practice;

(2) share their craft knowledge; (3) observe one another while they are engaged in practice; and (4) root for one another's success (Barth, 2006). As we examined the walkthrough process at the schools featured in this book, we noted that each had become a learning community. They had shifted the organization and structure of their professional development efforts toward integrating teacher learning into communities of shared practice. Teachers collaboratively examined their day-to-day practices to meet the educational needs of all their students. They viewed student success not as an individual effort but as a schoolwide effort.

Burlington High School is an excellent example of a school transforming into a learning community. Burlington's staff illustrated that they valued the process of learning by sharing their experiences with one another and engaging in meaningful discussions about what high-quality learning looks like. The success of their walkthroughs rests largely on widely held assumptions that staff members want to refine their practice and that improving teaching practice improves student learning. As part of a learning community, walkthroughs allow these high school teachers to

> Teachers need to value each other as professionals and be willing to work together to improve instruction and learning for all students.
>
> *—Mike Skelton,*
> *Principal, Jonesboro High School*

- Seek and share ideas, strategies, and resources with one another.
- Work together as a whole school toward improving student learning.
- Make public instructional practices that have been traditionally private.
- Engage in professional, collective, reflective inquiry that contributes to improving teaching practices for improved student outcomes.

The principal at Basalt Middle School stressed the importance of a culture in which teachers are actively and collaboratively engaged as a community of learners. He said that teachers see one another as resources for their own professional growth; they are better able to share a common vision, recognize that learning occurs in a context of taking action, and see engagement and experience as the most effective "teachers." The principal at Griffith Elementary School concurred by pointing out how critical it is to student success that teachers be willing to collaborate as a learning community, sharing best practices and remaining open-minded and nonjudgmental in their efforts to grow together professionally.

Collaborative Inquiry

Collaborative inquiry is another component of a culture that welcomes walkthroughs. Collaborative inquiry occurs when teachers work together to identify common challenges, analyze relevant data, and suggest and test instructional approaches (David, 2007–08). Teachers reflect on the relationship between their classroom practices and student performance. Collaborative inquiry can improve the instructional capacity of teachers and strengthen the decision making that supports student improvement. It reflects a cultural openness to the examination of better ways of doing things—even those practices that are a significant departure from the past (Danielson, 2006). When teachers have opportunities for collaborative inquiry and its related learning, the result is a body of wisdom about teaching that becomes widely shared. All of the educators and students in your school can benefit from this collective expertise.

> In order for schools to reap the greatest benefit from teacher walkthroughs, each teacher must be willing to collaborate with colleagues, reflect on his or her own practice, and be ready to embark on professional conversations that will challenge one's own thinking while taking rigor to the next level. The results are obvious through student achievement.
>
> —*Kimberly Naiman,*
> *3rd/4th Grade Teacher,*
> *Arroyo Vista Charter School*

Benefits from teacher walkthrough data as part of collaborative inquiry generally include

- Evidence of student learning that affects instructional decisions.
- Adjustments to instruction and curriculum that meet students' specific learning needs.
- Cultivation within the school of responsibility for student performance.
- On-the-job professional development.
- Identification of schoolwide professional development needs.
- Improvement in student achievement.

Several walkthrough models include collaborative inquiry as an inherent component. Nelsen and Cudeiro (2009) refer to collaborative inquiry as "cycles of professional learning." The intent is to create a professional learning plan that builds expertise in all staff members through repeated cycles of high-quality learning. This cycle includes opportunities for practicing, receiving feedback, observing colleagues in walkthroughs, ongoing professional reading, and peer discussion. It also includes examining the effect of practices on student learning by looking at student work and reviewing student performance data. A powerful support in this cycle of learning comes from having teachers observe other teachers practicing a new strategy and then discussing in detail what was observed in those classrooms.

In the UCLA Center X Classroom Walk-Through Model, which is used by a number of schools, Patricia Martinez-Miller and Laureen Cervone (2008) refer to collaborative inquiry as a "cycle of continuous improvement." In this model, six elements determine the cycle of continuous improvement:

> The teacher walkthrough process is such an eye-opener to what is really going on at school. Many times we make assumptions, either good or bad, about what is happening inside our classrooms. The walkthrough provides a rare opportunity for our staff to put those assumptions aside and be proactive in discovering together the truth about student learning.
>
> —*Jennifer Ortiz, Professional Development Team member, South Junior High School, California*

1. Define a desired future: Clearly define what students are capable of achieving.
2. Gather data: Include evidence from state assessments, district benchmarks, classroom work, teacher professional knowledge, and teacher walkthroughs.
3. Hypothesize: Structure ideas about different ways of working with students that might have a positive influence on the behavior or outcome desired.
4. Implement: Try the suggested strategies in the classroom.
5. Reflect on implementation: Ensure that the improvement process includes time and settings to reflect on the evidence from what has been implemented.

6. Next steps: Refine and sustain implementation of strategies that are working.

Lessons Learned and Moving Forward

An expectation of the profession is to understand the importance of collaboration and how we owe it to our profession to help each other to grow.

—Elba Maisonet, former principal, Schubert Elementary School

Involving teachers in walkthroughs will succeed in a school where the culture features strong principal leadership, shared leadership, trust and safety for risk taking, a student-centered staff, a community of learning, and collaborative inquiry. The role of the school leadership is critical to the introduction, implementation, and sustenance of walkthroughs that actively involve teachers in the process. The principal is important in dealing with teacher concerns and providing resources to the process (for example, coordination of the walkthroughs and arrangements for discussions after the walks).

Shared leadership can create a vision for walkthroughs as a tool to promote reflective dialogue and growth around teaching and learning. In some schools, individual teacher leaders have taken responsibility for advocating for walkthroughs with one another. In other schools, it was the school leadership team that generated interest and helped with the implementation and monitoring of walkthroughs.

A culture of trust among all staff is essential for the successful implementation of walkthroughs. Trust occurs when teachers know that the walkthrough process is safe. They feel comfortable taking risks by trying out new instructional strategies and technologies without fear of criticism during walkthroughs.

Schools where students are at the center of the culture are excellent settings for walkthroughs. Students benefit when they are the primary focus of walkthroughs, and teachers work together to refine their instruction to better meet student needs. When students are at the center, the walkthrough focus is less likely to be on the teacher.

A school culture that reflects a community of learning invites walkthroughs. Communities of learning have a high level of professionalism, collegiality, and shared personal practice. Staff members exhibit a strong desire to refine their teaching practices by making a commitment to continual learning. These are schools where teachers engage in collaborative inquiry with one another, identify common challenges, analyze relevant walkthrough and other student data, and explore new instructional interventions that improve student performance.

Certain components of a school's culture contribute to a better environment for the successful implementation of classroom walkthroughs. When those characteristics are in play, teachers will embrace the positive outcomes of observing one another through walkthroughs—seeing themselves as professional colleagues who encourage and support one another's learning and growth, and serving in a school where the priority is achieving the highest standards of teaching and learning practices for all of its students.

Questions to Think About

- What components of your school's culture demonstrate readiness to implement walkthroughs?
- What features of your school culture may need to be adjusted to support walkthroughs?
- What support would the principal provide if walkthroughs were implemented in your school?
- How can teacher leaders or the school leadership team become advocates for generating interest in the teaching staff to participate in walkthroughs?
- How would you assess the level of trust and safety for risk taking in your school?
- In what ways is your school a community of learning? What else might be needed to create such a community?
- How would you rate the level of collaborative inquiry among teaching colleagues in your school?

Our Recommendations

- Solicit the commitment and support of school leaders for walkthroughs as an appropriate form of professional development.

- During the early stages of the walkthrough planning and implementation process, seek teachers who can influence other staff members about the process and its value.
- Have teachers on the school leadership team participate in the walkthrough process early, and ask them to share their experiences.
- Promote opportunities for teachers to join the walkthrough team early in the implementation process.
- Provide ways for all teachers to feel safe in expressing their thoughts and concerns regarding walkthroughs.
- Continually reinforce the idea that walkthroughs are professional growth opportunities for all teachers to become better at their craft.

CHAPTER 3

Components of Successful Walkthroughs

The single greatest influence on the professional practices of teachers is the direct observation of other teachers.

—Douglas B. Reeves

When considering the introduction of walkthroughs, the first decision to make is whether to implement an existing walkthrough model or develop a personalized model. The basic components of walkthroughs are the same in both cases. These components are the (1) protocol of the walkthrough (frequency of walkthrough observations, amount of time spent in each classroom, and so on); (2) participants engaged as observers in the walkthrough; (3) focus of the walkthrough (the general area of instruction, curriculum, or other aspects of the classroom environment to be observed) and the specific look-fors under each focus area; (4) data-gathering process (checklists, observation notes, and optional use of observation software); and (5) feedback or follow-up in a timely manner with individual teachers, groups of teachers, or the whole staff. In this chapter, we introduce you to the components of walkthroughs as used by the schools featured in our study.

Walkthrough Models

For each school (see Figure 3.1), we identified the walkthrough model used, the name used to identify the walkthrough process, and the number of years of walkthrough implementation through the 2011–2012 school year. Four schools began their first year of engaging teachers in walkthroughs in 2011–2012, whereas quite a number of schools already had five or more years of implementation at that point.

FIGURE 3.1
Walkthrough Models, Names, and Years of Implementation

School	Walkthrough Model	Walkthrough Name	Years Implemented*
Alan Shawn Feinstein Middle School (Rhode Island)	Locally designed**	Literacy Walks	5
Arroyo Vista Charter School (California)	Locally designed	Instructional Walkthroughs	13
Ball Junior High School (California)	UCLA Center X Classroom Walk-Through	Classroom Walkthroughs (CWTs)	3
Basalt Middle School (Colorado)	McREL Power Walkthrough	Walkthroughs (WTs)	4
Belleville East High School (Illinois)	Instructional Practices Inventory (IPI) Process	Instructional Practices Inventory (IPI)	3
Belleville West High School (Illinois)	Instructional Practices Inventory (IPI) Process	Instructional Practices Inventory (IPI)	4
Benton Grade School K–4 (Illinois)	Locally designed	Classroom Walkthroughs	1
Bridges High School (Colorado)	McREL Power Walkthrough	Walkthroughs (WTs)	7
Burlington High School (Massachusetts)	Look 2 Learning	Learning Walks	3
Cheney Middle School (Washington)	Locally designed	Walkthroughs	7
Cleveland High School (Washington)	Data-in-a-Day	Data-in-a-Day	5

School	Walkthrough Model	Walkthrough Name	Years Implemented*
Crownhill Elementary School (Washington)	Locally designed	Learning Walks	7
Crystal River Elementary School (Colorado)	McREL Power Walkthrough	Walkthroughs (WTs)	3
DeWitt Perry Middle School (Texas)	Instructional Rounds (City et al.)	Campus-Based Walkthroughs	1
Dr. Charles E. Murphy Elementary School (Connecticut)	UCLA Center X Classroom Walk-Through	Professional Learning Visits (PLVs)	2
Edmonton Public Schools (Canada)	Locally designed	Instructional Talk-Throughs	6
E. R. Geddes Elementary School (California)	UCLA Center X Classroom Walk-Through	Classroom Walkthroughs	8
Fontana School District (California)	Locally designed	Instructional Walkthroughs	3
Fort Vancouver High School (Washington)	Locally designed	Buildingwide Learning Walks	3
Ganado Intermediate School (Arizona)	Locally designed	Formative Observations	3
Griffith Elementary School (Tennessee)	Instructional Rounds (Marzano)	Instructional Rounds	2
Huntingtown High School (Maryland)	Locally designed	Walkthroughs	2
James Hubert Blake High School (Maryland)	Locally designed	Walkthroughs	5
Jonesboro High School (Arkansas)	Teachscape Reflect Classroom Walkthrough	Peer Observations	3
Katella High School (California)	Locally designed	Classroom Focus Walks (CFWs)	3
Lancaster High School (California)	Locally designed	Classroom Walkthroughs	9
Leonard J. Tyl Middle School (Connecticut)	UCLA Center X Classroom Walk-Through	Professional Learning Visits (PLVs)	2
M. L. King, Jr. Middle School (Maryland)	Learning Walk Routine	Learning Walks	5

continued

FIGURE 3.1

Walkthrough Models, Names, and Years of Implementation (*continued*)

School	Walkthrough Model	Walkthrough Name	Years Implemented*
Mohegan Elementary School (Connecticut)	UCLA Center X Classroom Walk-Through	Professional Learning Visits (PLVs)	2
Monitor Elementary School (Arkansas)	Locally designed	Classroom Walkthroughs (CWTs)	5
Munford Elementary School (Alabama)	Instructional Rounds (City et al.)	Instructional Rounds	1
Oxford Academy (California)	Locally designed	Student Learning Walks	2
Parkway Elementary School (Connecticut)	UCLA Center X Classroom Walk-Through	Classroom Walkthroughs (CWTs)	6
Randels Elementary School (Michigan)	McREL Power Walkthrough	Walkthroughs	4
Salt Creek Elementary School (California)	Locally designed	Walkthroughs	6
Schubert Elementary School (Illinois)	Locally designed	Instructional Rounds	4
South Junior High School (California)	UCLA Center X Classroom Walk-Through	Classroom Walkthroughs (CWTs)	4
South Junior High School (Idaho)	Look 2 Learning	L2L Walks, or Walks	2
Summit Middle School (Indiana)	Locally designed	Collaborative Learning Visits (CLVs)	1
Williamsport Area High School (Pennsylvania)	Locally designed	Learning Walks	2

* Years implemented through the 2011–2012 school year.

** "Locally designed" is the term used to describe a model created by the school or district to best meet its needs and goals.

We refer to walkthroughs, but a number of schools use other labels, such as "instructional rounds," "instructional talk-throughs," "learning walks," "classroom focus walks," "literacy walks," and "professional learning visits." One reason schools select other labels is to avoid any connection to supervision or evaluation. They want the purpose of the walkthrough to be clearly defined by its label as a school improvement effort and on-site professional development opportunity. However, we believe the label given to the process is less important than a strong assurance that the walkthroughs involving teachers are nonevaluative, well-planned professional learning experiences, and consistently aligned to the stated purpose and expected outcomes.

Our review of the schools involving teachers in walkthroughs demonstrates that at least nine different regionally or nationally known walkthrough models were implemented. The other schools designed their own walkthrough protocols. Figure 3.2 presents a comparison of these national or regional walkthrough models, and Appendix D provides source information for each of them.

Locally designed classroom walkthrough models are those developed by individual districts or schools to meet their specific needs and goals. Monitor Elementary School offers one example of a locally designed walkthrough model. The school administration and teachers created their own protocol for classroom walkthroughs (which they abbreviate as CWT) with the general purpose of increasing the professional growth of teachers. The specific focus of each walkthrough changes according to the particular best-practice strategy the faculty is implementing. All classroom teachers participate in the walks and are observed. A cohort of teachers, administrators, or instructional facilitators conduct the CWTs at least once a month for a 35-minute period, visiting four to seven classrooms for about five minutes each during that time. After each round of CWTs, participants engage in a 10-minute reflective conversation to review data collected during the walks and to discuss what they gained from the experience. The specific focus is determined in conjunction with the principal and is based on the collection of data from prior walks, student achievement data, current professional growth initiatives, or a combination of those elements. Participants use a graphic organizer, a rubric, or both for taking notes during each walk. The forms are created for each particular CWT, and the collection of data and reflective conversations are focused on the specific purpose for the walk. Observation notes are handwritten, and the observer keeps his or her notes and gives a copy to the principal. The principal compiles the data and presents a summary to the school leadership team to determine future

FIGURE 3.2

Comparison of National and Regional Walkthrough Models

Model	Purpose/Use	Participants	Focus/Look-fors	Data Gathering	Feedback/Follow-up
Data-in-a-Day	One day of structured visits to observe, collect, and compile data, and reflect on data in an effort to strengthen teaching and learning. Data-in-a-Day typically occurs three times annually.	All classrooms are visited by a four-person team, usually consisting of parents, teachers, and students.	Four focus questions from the Motivation Framework for Culturally Responsive Teaching guide the observed look-fors.	Teams are provided with a form of rubrics around the Motivation Framework so they can note what to observe across the classrooms visited. Each team visits six classrooms for 15 minutes each.	Teams summarize and analyze their observation data. Teams then share their observations and recommendations with building staff for further reflection and action.
Instructional Practices Inventory (IPI)	A one-day process for creating an optimum profile of student engagement in learning that serves as the basis for collaborative faculty study and subsequent refinement of how students are engaged in learning throughout the school. Schools typically collect data three times a year.	Data collection is completed by teachers from the school or school leaders from other schools (usually not including building administrators). Participants must be trained on how to codify student engagement on the six IPI categories used for observation.	Six coding categories under the broad categories of Student-Engaged Instruction, Teacher-Directed Instruction, and Disengagement determine the focus and look-fors.	Teams use an observation rubric for recording data on observed student engagement.	Summarized student engagement profiles are provided to the entire school staff to collaboratively study and reflect upon their perceptions of effective learning and instruction.

Model	Purpose/Use	Participants	Focus/Look-fors	Data Gathering	Feedback/Follow-up
Instructional Rounds Network	Usually monthly visits, each time at a different school, to acquire an understanding of what is happening in classrooms, how the system produces those effects, and how the school system or individual schools can move closer to the desired learning outcomes.	A network of superintendents, principals, teachers, and central office staff agree to meet each time at a different school. They spend the morning circulating around classrooms, observing the teaching and learning that take place.	Observations are based on a "problem of practice" the school has committed to solve, such as improving math proficiency or literacy. In general, this should be a major component of the school's improvement plan.	Observing teams are "scripting" to collect evidence on the state of teaching in the building.	In the debriefing meeting, members are further asked to take four steps: (1) describe what they observed in classes; (2) analyze any patterns that emerge; (3) predict the kind of learning they might expect from the teaching observed; and (4) recommend the next level of work that could help the school better achieve its improvement goals.
Instructional Rounds	Observing teachers to compare their own instructional practices with those of the teachers they observe.	Small groups of three to five teachers, and the lead teacher, make relatively brief observations of their fellow teachers. All teachers should have a chance to participate at least once a semester.	Observations are based on The Art and Science of Teaching (Marzano, 2007), which is a comprehensive framework for effective instruction. Ten design questions are used by teachers to plan effective units and lessons within those units.	Observing teachers use the Marzano Observational Protocol Snapshot form.	Members of the observing team convene to debrief on their experiences. Debriefing should end with all observers identifying one thing they will do differently in their classroom as a result of the rounds. Feedback to teachers observed is not provided unless requested.

continued

FIGURE 3.2

Comparison of National and Regional Walkthrough Models (*continued*)

Model	Purpose/Use	Participants	Focus/Look-fors	Data Gathering	Feedback/Follow-up
Learning Walk Routine	Develop a common language and vision of teaching and learning using the Institute for Learning's Principles of Learning. Focus of classroom observations is on what students learn.	Administrators and teachers observe individually or as teams.	Focus is on one or more of nine Principles of Learning that are condensed theoretical statements summarizing decades of learning research. They are designed to help educators analyze the quality of instruction and opportunities for learning that they offer to students.	Observers record their observations on an open-ended form that enables them to record any type of evidence. They do not draw conclusions on what they observed but rather record wonderings and thought-provoking questions for reflection and action.	Observation data are shared with the staff so they can analyze, reflect, and plan for the enhancement of their instructional expertise aligned to the nine Principles of Learning and the engagement and achievement of their students.
Look 2 Learning	A research-based tool that allows schools to improve student achievement, generate data on learning, focus school improvement efforts, and begin discussions about improving classroom practices. Focus is on student learning and speaking to students about what they are doing during class in order to gather school-wide trend data.	Administrators and teachers observe individually or as teams.	Focus incorporates the latest research on student achievement and engagement, specifically asking (1) Is the objective of the lesson clear to the students? (2) What is the level of critical thinking on Bloom's taxonomy? and (3) What is the level of student engagement (Engaged, Compliant, or Off-Task)?	Observers use simple recording forms as well as a Look 2 Learning software option that provides an electronic way to collect and send data to a web-based analysis program.	Through the collection and sharing of cumulative, anonymous data, teachers in grade-level teams, departments, or professional learning communities are empowered to analyze and reflect on classroom trends.

Model	Purpose/Use	Participants	Focus/Look-fors	Data Gathering	Feedback/Follow-up
McREL Power Walkthrough	To provide educators with strategies for using an informal observation approach and data to inform reflective feedback as a vehicle for maximizing student achievement. The focus of observations is on students.	Administrators and teachers observe individually or as teams.	Focus and look-fors center on the extent to which teachers use instructional strategies from *Classroom Instruction That Works*; the use of technology in the classroom and the level of student engagement; the level of instructional rigor, as measured by Bloom's taxonomy; the context of instruction (e.g., whole group, cooperative groups, pairs); and the indicators of learning (e.g., peer teaching, student writing, simulating/modeling).	Observers use Power Walkthrough software, based on McREL's *Classroom Instruction That Works* research-based instructional strategies, which can be loaded on wireless devices.	Reports enable a school to share observations with teachers individually or at grade/team meetings for subsequent coaching conversations and reflective questioning.
Teachscape *Reflect* **Classroom Walkthrough**	An iterative process to collect and analyze data about the quality of instruction, the level of student engagement, and the rigor of the curriculum. The walkthrough process promotes focused dialogue about teaching and learning and is a continuous improvement process that translates data into practical actions steps.	Principals, assistant principals, coaches, and teachers conduct observations.	Includes a standard set of look-fors based on leading research for effective instruction (High-Yield Strategies, Bloom's Taxonomy, Student Engagement, Instructional Methods and Resources, Learning Environment, and Differentiation). Because every educational setting is unique, look-fors can be created and customized to address a district's specific needs.	Observers use Teachscape Reflect Classroom Walkthrough, a data collection, analysis, and reporting system for brief, targeted classroom observations. This system can be used on a variety of handheld wireless devices.	Professional learning communities or grade-level teams meet over the classroom walkthrough data to reflect on what's happening in the classroom from a variety of perspectives and plan improvement efforts.

continued

FIGURE 3.2

Comparison of National and Regional Walkthrough Models *(continued)*

Model	Purpose/Use	Participants	Focus/Look-fors	Data Gathering	Feedback/Follow-up
UCLA Center X Classroom Walk-Through	To enable teachers to acquire a greater understanding of the results of their current instructional practices and implement the kind of changes to improve practices that result in significant student achievement. Students are the focus of the observations.	Classroom teachers are the primary participants in the walkthroughs. They form teams of five or fewer to visit classrooms.	A focus question to guide teacher team observations is identified by the school based on the improvement initiatives already underway at the school and in the district.	Observers record what they observe and hear on an observation graphic without adding any interpretations.	Observers convene to debrief the trends or patterns in student learning based on evidence collected about the focus question. The staff explore together the evidence collected, reflect on its meaning, and decide on next steps.

professional development for individuals, grade levels, or the entire faculty. Only the principal delivers observation feedback to individual teachers.

Another example of a locally designed walkthrough model takes place at Alan Shawn Feinstein Middle School. Walks at Feinstein are conducted every two to three months to determine the degree to which teachers are effectively implementing formative assessment. Teacher observers use a checklist to gather data, and the school staff uses the feedback to review their formative assessment practices, adjust instruction, and plan for future professional development and resource supports.

Feinstein Middle School's Literacy Action Team leads the walkthroughs. For each walk, five teachers from the team are anchors—those always present to maintain the integrity and consistency of the process. Five additional teachers participate with the anchors during walks. The non-team teacher participants are continually rotated so all teachers have an opportunity for walkthrough observations. At the end of the walkthrough day, all participants take part in a discussion to summarize their observations, analyze the data collected, and determine recommendations and next steps. A one-page report documenting this discussion goes to the entire faculty and is followed with professional development targeted to one or more of the recommendations.

Instructional Talk-Through (ITT) is an ongoing classroom-embedded professional development experience that was locally designed by six collaborating schools in the K–9 Edmonton Public Schools. The purpose of ITT is to help teachers improve teaching practices, increase student engagement, and use assessment practices that enhance student success. It is an intervisitation process in which each school hosts teacher teams from other schools. The teams visit a selected number of classrooms within the host school for 15 to 20 minutes each. This protocol is unique in that the host teachers share their instructional focus with the visiting teams before they arrive. The sharing helps the visitors focus their observations on the intended strategies. Teachers trained to facilitate the ITT process help with the post-observation discussions between hosting teachers and visiting teams (Cronk et al., 2008).

Protocol: Observers, Frequency, and Length of Observations

Most of the schools we studied involve all of their classroom teachers in walkthroughs. Some, however, open the process to those who volunteer as observers rather than require participation by everyone. In other schools, only those teachers trained in a given walkthrough protocol are allowed to participate as observers; and in a few schools, the initial set of observers includes only instructional coaches, mentors, the school leadership team, or a special committee of teachers who oversee the teacher walkthrough process.

> Teachers leading teachers is the best model for implementing teacher walkthroughs.
>
> —*Suzanne Lacey, Superintendent of Schools, Talladega County Schools*

Some observers are teamed horizontally with colleagues from the same grade level or subject to walk together. Other schools mix teams vertically to represent teachers from various grades or curricular areas. In some cases, teams visit every classroom; in others, teams visit a designated number of classrooms.

Some walkthroughs are designed for teachers to walk and observe alone. In other circumstances, teachers accompany an administrator or a group as part of the observation team. Individual team members might assume different observation responsibilities. For example, one person might just observe the teacher; another, just the students; and another, student products or artifacts displayed on the walls. Several schools use a team member as a timekeeper during observations to let others know when the visit is completed. All of these variations relate to the specific purpose or intended outcome of the walkthroughs.

Although the frequency of walks ranged from once a week to once a year, schools typically conducted walkthroughs quarterly. Observation time in each classroom ranged from one or two minutes to 25 minutes. In most schools, the observation time was 10 minutes or less. Figure 3.3 summarizes the frequency and length of walks and the participants in each school's walkthrough.

FIGURE 3.3

Observers, Frequency, and Length of Observations

School	Frequency	Length (minutes)	Observers
Alan Shawn Feinstein Middle School (Rhode Island)	Every 2–3 months	Varies	Literacy Action Team and volunteer teachers
Arroyo Vista Charter School (California)	Quarterly	4–7	Instructional Leadership Team, all classroom teachers, principal, and assistant principal
Ball Junior High School (California)	3 times annually	5–7	Volunteering classroom teachers
Basalt Middle School (Colorado)	Quarterly	3–5	All classroom teachers
Belleville East High School (Illinois)	Twice per semester	1–2	Teachers trained in the IPI process
Belleville West High School (Illinois)	3–4 times annually	1–3	Teachers trained in the IPI process
Benton Grade School K–4 (Illinois)	3 times annually	5	School leadership team members, volunteering teachers, and principal
Bridges High School (Colorado)	Weekly	3–5	All classroom teachers
Burlington High School (Massachusetts)	Once a week	3–5	Volunteering teachers and all school leadership
Cheney Middle School (Washington)	Twice annually	25	Teacher leaders from each grade level (6–8)
Cleveland High School (Washington)	Twice annually	20	Teams of visitors (includes teachers, parents/community members, students)
Crownhill Elementary School (Washington)	Twice annually	10–20	All classroom teachers (can include instructional coach)
Crystal River Elementary School (Colorado)	Twice annually	3–5	Building Leadership Team and other interested teachers
DeWitt Perry Middle School (Texas)	1–2 times monthly	20	Instructional Leadership Team (four department chairs) and four instructional facilitators (teachers)
Dr. Charles E. Murphy Elementary School (Connecticut)	3–4 times annually	5	One trained teacher from K, 1st, 3rd, and 4th grades and one from music

continued

FIGURE 3.3
Observers, Frequency, and Length of Observations *(continued)*

School	Frequency	Length (minutes)	Observers
Edmonton Public Schools (Alberta, Canada)	1–2 times annually	20	All classroom teachers
E. R. Geddes Elementary School (California)	1–2 times annually	15	Site leadership team, volunteering classroom teachers, and parents
Fontana School District (California)	Once annually	Varies	All newly hired classroom teachers
Fort Vancouver High School (Washington)	Quarterly	5–15	All classroom teachers including student teachers and staff assistants
Ganado Intermediate School (Arizona)	Weekly	10–15	Academic coach, three mentor teachers, and school principal
Griffith Elementary School (Tennessee)	Twice annually	15	All classroom teachers and principal
Huntingtown High School (Maryland)	Quarterly	10	All classroom teachers
James Hubert Blake High School (Maryland)	Annually	25	All classroom teachers and counselors
Jonesboro High School (Arkansas)	Once a semester	10–20	All classroom teachers led by school's instructional strategist
Katella High School (California)	Once a quarter	7–10	Volunteer teachers facilitated by Lesson Design Specialist
Lancaster High School (California)	Twice annually	5–8	Teacher leaders, instructional coaches, and volunteering teachers
Leonard J. Tyl Middle School (Connecticut)	3 times annually	5–8	Any volunteering teachers across grade levels and content areas
M. L. King, Jr. Middle School (Maryland)	Quarterly	10–15	All classroom teachers
Mohegan Elementary School (Connecticut)	4 times annually	20	Volunteering classroom teachers
Monitor Elementary School (Arkansas)	1 day per week to 1 week per month	5	All certified staff, administrators, instructional facilitators, counselors, and SPED staff
Munford Elementary School (Alabama)	Monthly	10–12	Team comprising administrator, reading coach, and observation-trained teachers
Oxford Academy (California)	Once a quarter	10–15	Lesson Design Team (volunteers representing all curricular areas) led by Lesson Design Coach

School	Frequency	Length (minutes)	Observers
Parkway Elementary School (Connecticut)	3–4 times annually	7–10	All certified staff members
Randels Elementary School (Michigan)	Weekly	3–5	Interested classroom teachers, principal, and central office staff member
Salt Creek Elementary School (California)	Once a quarter	10–15	All classroom teachers
Schubert Elementary School (Illinois)	2–3 times annually	5–10	Instructional Leadership Team
South Junior High School (California)	1–2 times annually	5–7	CWT-trained teachers, volunteer teachers, and counselors
South Junior High School (Idaho)	Twice a month	2–4	Classroom teachers trained in the L2L model
Summit Middle School (Indiana)	Quarterly	6–10	Volunteering classroom teachers, principals
Williamsport Area High School (Pennsylvania)	2–3 times monthly	5	Building Leadership Team, counselors, librarian, aides, any volunteering teachers

Walkthrough Focus and Look-fors

What distinguishes walkthroughs from other informal classroom observations is the fact that the observations have a specific focus and a definite set of look-fors under each area of focus. The walkthrough focus supports school improvement goals. Schools can draw from a wide range of sources to identify the walkthrough focus and look-fors. The schools we studied identified the following areas as sources for focus areas and look-fors:

- Student performance data
- Research on effective teaching and learning
- Professional development training
- Curricular and instructional initiatives
- School improvement plans
- Districtwide improvement plans
- School district strategic plan
- State learning standards and policies
- Data from previous walkthroughs
- Feedback from teacher surveys

Of course, it is important to continuously evaluate, adjust, and change the focus of walkthroughs as additional data become available.

Schools shared some specific examples of focus areas they chose, including the following:

- Equitable teaching practices
- Differentiated instruction
- Guided reading
- Writing across the curriculum
- Reading across the curriculum
- Literacy instruction
- Formative assessment
- Response to Intervention (RTI)
- Student engagement
- Learning styles
- Higher-order questioning
- Use of technology
- Classroom management
- Learning environment
- Evidence of learning

A focus area can be a descriptive statement or it can be a guiding observation question for teacher observers. Schools using the UCLA Center X Classroom Walk-Through model ask, "What questions are we seeking to answer from walkthroughs about teaching and learning in our school?" The criteria for developing an effective focus question should (1) center on the instructional practices of the teacher or on what students understand and are doing—or both; (2) be open-ended enough to allow possibilities to emerge that had not been considered initially; (3) be about discovering rather than measuring; (4) be answered by observations, descriptions, and interactions; and (5) generate data that will provide information about progress toward a stated goal (Linsley, Martinez-Miller, & Tambara, 2011). Here are some examples of focus questions:

- What evidence demonstrates that we are using effective questioning techniques to assist students in developing high-level thinking?
- What inquiry-based laboratory activities are our students using to learn science content?
- What evidence shows that our instruction is more student-centered than teacher-centered?
- What evidence do we see that formative assessments are being used to track student learning of the Common Core State Standards?

- How are our English language learners adjusting and actively engaging in classroom learning experiences?
- How is technology being integrated into our daily instruction and student learning?
- What evidence illustrates that we are integrating the Common Core State Standards into our curricular and instructional strategies?

After a school has determined and agreed on the focus of the walkthrough, it creates look-fors to narrow the focus into manageable chunks for observation. We define look-fors as those explicit teacher or student behaviors that teachers will observe and record throughout their walks. Look-fors are clear statements or descriptors of evidence of teaching and learning that relate directly to the focus. Examples of look-fors are specific instructional strategies, learning activities, behavioral outcomes, artifacts or displays, routines, or practices (Kachur et al., 2010). It is extremely important to have a common understanding and consistent set of look-fors by both the observers and the observed. In Figure 3.4, we present an example from the walkthrough protocol at James Hubert Blake High School showing three focus areas and their associated look-fors related to both teacher and student behaviors.

> As a teacher, you benefit from seeing firsthand what works for your peers and what does not. We are more confident and less resistant to implementing a new instructional strategy if we have personally observed successful delivery of that strategy in an unrehearsed classroom setting.
>
> *—Becky Darby, Math Teacher,*
> *Jonesboro High School*

Appendix E summarizes the sources schools have drawn upon for the selection of their focus areas for observation. Teachers must be given the opportunity to help identify the specific area or areas of focus for walkthroughs and the accompanying look-fors. In fact, the full participation of all teachers in the development and implementation of the entire walkthrough process will help ensure their understanding and support and the success of this endeavor. Teachers are professionals regarding what is to be implemented and observed in the classroom to foster improved student learning.

FIGURE 3.4
Three Focus Areas and Associated Look-fors

Expectations	Classroom Climate	Personal Relationships
The teacher . . . • verbalizes high expectations and pushes students to higher levels of performance. • communicates objectives and purpose. • makes connections. • checks for understanding and provides specific feedback. • uses equitable practices (random calling, etc.).	The teacher . . . • encourages and supports students in a welcoming classroom. • provides a safe environment where students are comfortable taking risks. • shows passion for the subject. • provides opportunities for student discourse.	The teacher . . . • uses students' names. • asks students about their lives. • makes personal connections. • uses personal anecdotes to build background knowledge.
The student . . . • knows and follows established routines. • asks questions and responds to questions. • focuses on learning, completing tasks as requested. • prepares for class, has materials ready, and completes homework.	The student . . . • asks questions and makes connections. • supports his or her classmates' ideas. • works cooperatively, participating in group discussions/tasks. • respects other students and the teacher.	The student . . . • appears comfortable sharing personal stories. • answers questions freely. • respects and values the opinions of others. • comes to class prepared and ready to participate.

Source: Used with permission from James Hubert Blake High School, Silver Spring, Maryland.

Gathering Walkthrough Data

Different walkthrough models use various means to gather data. Most use some type of observation form to record information. We classify these forms into three types: (1) a checklist of look-fors; (2) a checklist with space for written comments; and (3) a form with space for written comments only. Again, like other aspects of walkthroughs, the type of form you use will be determined by the purpose and expected outcomes of your walkthroughs. Some forms include teachers' names, and others guard their privacy.

The teachers at Huntingtown High School use a checklist of look-fors (Figure 3.5) in the walkthrough observations of fellow teachers and students. Teachers are required to do at least one walkthrough per quarter. For one quarter, they may observe classes within their own department; the next quarter, they may observe the same students they teach but in subject areas other than their own; and for the other two quarters, they have the option to go anywhere else outside their department.

An example of a combination checklist and space for written notes is the form used at Ganado Intermediate School, a Native American school in Ganado, Arizona, serving grades 4 through 6 (see Figure 3.6). Teachers use an 11-item checklist observation form to determine which research-based skills are evident during their 10–15 minute classroom walkthrough visits. The last item on the checklist is about student engagement. Observers may ask individual students about what they are learning; why the lesson is important to them and how they think the lesson relates to their lives.

Being on both sides of the walkthrough is important. Every time I am in a teacher's classroom, I learn something new, whether it is something new I want to put into practice or something that has been brought to my attention that is not good practice.

—Cindy Stubbs, Language Arts Teacher,
DeWitt Perry Middle School

Some observation forms include just a focus question and space for written comments. Teachers at Parkway Elementary School use a T-chart (see Figure 3.7) to collect information during observations. The focus question is written at the top of the form. In the left column, walkthrough participants record their observations about student behavior and the learning environment related to the focus question. In the right column, they record questions to clarify their understanding of what they observe.

Teacher observers at Mohegan Elementary School use three-by-three-inch sticky notes to record their observations, using a separate note for every piece of observed evidence of the focus. When walkthrough teams meet to debrief their observations, they place the sticky notes on a chart titled "Problem of Practice," which refers to the problem they identified as their focus. Placement of these sticky notes into categories on the chart or wall enables immediate identification of patterns, making a compelling visual to facilitate discussion. Walkthrough teams use these notes as preparation for feedback to share with the teachers observed.

FIGURE 3.5
Walkthrough Checklist 1

Class _____ Period _____

Classroom Activities Observed

____ Lecture/Note Taking

____ Quiz/Test

____ Whole-Group Discussion

____ Silent Reading

____ Working in Pairs

____ Oral Reading

____ Small Groups

____ Labs

____ Student Presentation/Performance Assessment

____ Games/Hands-on Activity

____ Movie/Film Clip

____ Exit Slips

____ Worksheet/Book Work

____ Questioning Students

____ Other _____

If questioning of students was observed, please check the level of questions you observed:

____ Knowledge Based (Who or what is. . . ?)

____ Analysis (What is the problem or issue?)

____ Comprehension (Put in your own words.)

____ Synthesis (What changes would you make?)

____ Application (How would you use it?)

____ Evaluation (What is your opinion?)

Source: Used with permission from Huntingtown High School, Huntingtown, Maryland.

FIGURE 3.6
Walkthrough Checklist 2

Teacher:		Grade:		Subject:	
Date:		Begin Time:		End Time:	
Behavior	**Yes**	**No**	**Comment(s)**		
Objectives posted for students					
Students engaged/ on-task					
Students respond in complete sentences					
Teacher feedback appropriate					
Teacher circulates the classroom					

Behavior	Yes	No	Comment(s)
Students grouped for instruction			
Teacher talk dominates lesson			
Classroom environment is orderly			
Teacher verified student understanding of lesson/task			
Higher level of questions used in discussion/lesson			
Student(s) can identify lesson objective and state why it is important			

Source: Used with permission from Ganado Intermediate School, Ganado, Arizona.

FIGURE 3.7
UCLA Center X Walk-Through Graphic Organizer

Date _____ Subject _____ Grade Level _____

Focus Question: _____

_____

Observations	Questions—Clarifying and Probing

Source: Used with permission from UCLA Center X, Trumbull, Connecticut.

Walkthrough Observation Software

One of the major challenges to making the most of walkthroughs is collecting, storing, and presenting the data. We know that using clipboards with checklists, index cards, or sheets of paper for notes can become cumbersome and require additional steps to analyze and report summaries of observations. We have found that technology has helped a number of schools make all of these chores much easier by reducing the number of steps it takes to conduct a teacher walkthrough and analyze the results.

With all of the advances in mobile handheld devices, there is an ever-growing array of software programs and mobile apps that are designed to make collection, storage, and presentation of walkthrough data easier. A number of these software programs (such as Austin Sky, Creighton TS4 Observation Instrument from WestEd, Teach for Success, eCOVE, iObservation system, ISTE Classroom Observation Tool, iWalkthrough, McREL PowerWalkthrough, Teachscape *Reflect* Classroom Walkthrough, observe4success, and Walk'bout) enable educators to upload walkthrough data to a website or download data to a device for later review and analysis. Most of these programs and apps allow the observer to record what is actually seen and heard during the walkthrough. In other words, the data collected are objective—evidence about an area of focus that is either apparent or not—and nonjudgmental.

Staff at Jonesboro High School use the Teachscape software. Aggregate reports that illustrate grade and subject comparisons and trends of instructional practice are created for the school and district. Staff members examine data about teaching practices, analyze data to measure progress toward school goals, and translate the data into the next action steps for the school.

The administrative team at Crystal River Elementary School uses a district-provided iPod Touch to record observations on a McREL template. The McREL walkthrough template is also used at Basalt Middle School, Bridges High School, and Randels Elementary School. These schools use the template on iPads® and customize the indicators to include their school improvement strategies.

The technology for recording observation data has dramatically accelerated with the expansion of various devices such as the iPad. The ability to use technology for automated data collection and immediate feedback for reflection is key to making short, frequent observations practical. This technology provides quick summary reports of observed patterns of teaching and learning across classrooms. Such data can then be better analyzed at the individual classroom level, grade level, department or subject area, or across the school as a whole. We believe that this approach greatly enhances the staff's ability to analyze walkthrough data in order to make quicker decisions about the changes most needed to improve teaching practices and student learning.

Walkthrough Follow-up

We share the opinion that for classroom walkthroughs to be successful, what happens after the walk is what improves teaching and learning. The greatest value of walkthroughs comes from sharing observation data via reflective conversations and taking subsequent actions to improve teaching and learning. Thoughtful questions encourage meaningful dialogue and deeper thinking about lessons, curricula, instructional strategies, and student learning. This process enables teachers to better identify and analyze strategies and issues. The goal is for all teachers to move toward self-reflection, self-analysis, and self-direction in the choices they make as they teach (Downey, Steffy, Poston, & English, 2010).

We emphasize the importance of teachers as critical participants in determining the purpose and format of the walkthrough follow-up. They will be the ones using walkthrough data to inform their instruction. In our study, we found a variety of ways in which follow-up is provided: (1) observers meeting directly with the staff (schoolwide, department, subject level, or grade level) to report and discuss data collected about an area of focus with no individual teacher feedback; (2) observers visiting face-to-face with individual teachers observed to provide feedback; (3) a combination of observers providing whole-staff feedback in terms of schoolwide patterns and practices observed and delivering individual teacher feedback; (4) written communication including handwritten notes, e-mails, or printed forms, such as letters or newsletters to the faculty; (5) summary reports automatically generated from software or mobile apps; and

(6) no feedback provided—the observing teachers discuss observations among themselves and think about how these observations would affect their own teaching decisions.

Group Feedback

Walkthrough feedback in many schools is presented to groups of teachers (departments, grades, or subject levels) or to the entire staff. These feedback meetings are collaborative and sometimes include a facilitator to assist with interpretation and reflection on the data and planning of next steps. The purpose of most whole-group feedback is to determine the patterns or trends of observed practices. Figure 3.8 shows a summary of observations found in the Literacy Walk Report of Alan Shawn Feinstein Middle School. Sharing these data with teachers allows them to reflect on their own practice and contributes to next steps in the formative assessment process.

> For the reflective teacher, observation is a very powerful motivator.
>
> —*Cheryl DeNosky, Reading Specialist, K–2nd grade, Benton Grade School K-4*

Teacher teams at Ball Junior High School meet after walks to chart observations in preparation for staff presentations. The teams look for patterns in the data and pose questions from the observations. At staff meetings, teachers discuss the data to determine if school goals are being achieved. Teachers discuss what they learn from the data and what they still need to learn to do. They also brainstorm next steps to help guide decisions regarding future professional development opportunities.

The teaching staff at South Junior High School in Idaho like the process for sharing observations from teacher walks that is part of the Look 2 Learning (L2L) walkthrough model—the "Four *R*s of Reflection." Initially, all of the data are shared with the staff. The four *R*s process gives the staff a framework for **r**estating, **r**eacting, **r**emembering, and **r**esponding to that data. The data can be further reviewed by grade level, subject area, or professional learning community teams. This process enables the staff to make decisions about future focus areas for walkthroughs and subsequent professional development.

FIGURE 3.8
Literacy Walk Report

SHARED LEARNING TARGET: Shared Learning Target is clearly articulated and understood by all students. Observation: • Most classrooms (95% or 52/55) had posted Shared Learning Target(s). • Some teachers verbally communicated Shared Learning Target with students in addition to posting it. • Few teachers referred to the Shared Learning Targets throughout the lesson. **Recommendation:** Refer to Shared Learning Target(s) throughout the lesson and return to it in your closure (e.g., summarize the lesson using the same language of the Shared Learning Target).	✔
STRATEGY: Formative assessment strategy (strategies) employed assessed student learning relative to the Shared Learning Target. Observation: • Most teachers (97%) applied formative assessment strategies related to the Shared Learning Targets (e.g., conferencing, observation, questioning, color-coded cups, entrance and exit slips, sticks, clickers, organizers, warm-ups, post-its, whiteboards, quick writes, quick draws, etc.). **Commendation:** Teachers are refining and expanding their use of formative assessment strategies, and some are using them multiple times throughout the lesson. Way to go! Keep up your efforts.	✔
INDIVIDUAL ASSESSMENT: Formative assessment strategy (strategies) assessed student performance at the individual level. Observation: • Most teachers (94%) assessed student performance at the individual level. **Commendation:** Many teachers assessed almost all students for accuracy or for understanding. Again, the faculty strives to employ best practices and support all students.	✔
FEEDBACK: Constructive feedback is provided to students. Observation: • Many teachers (77%) provide constructive feedback to students. **Recommendation:** Continue to provide constructive feedback (conferencing, press-back, follow-up questions, specific written feedback on paper or post-its, peer tutoring, peer editing, etc.) multiple times throughout the class.	✔

continued

FIGURE 3.8
Literacy Walk Report (*continued*)

OPPORTUNITY: Students are provided with an opportunity to use the feedback to do their work. Observation: • Many teachers (60%) provided opportunities for students to use the feedback to improve and/or revise their work. **Recommendation:** Continue to provide opportunities (class time, RTI Block, HW, etc.) for students to improve their work after providing them with constructive feedback.	✔
ADJUSTMENT: Minor and major lesson adjustments are made based on formative assessment results. Observation: • Many teachers (63%) adjusted instruction based upon formative assessment. **Recommendation:** Strategically adjust instruction throughout the lesson for all students (differentiated instruction, flexible grouping, etc.).	✔

Source: Used with permission from Alan Shawn Feinstein Middle School, Coventry, Rhode Island.

The teachers who participate in walkthroughs at Parkway Elementary School follow a very specific set of steps for preparing and giving feedback to the school faculty. The 10-step process consists of the following components:

1. Individually sharing what walkers observe.
2. Charting the information shared.
3. Looking for patterns and trends in the information recorded.
4. Listing patterns and trends.
5. Listing clarifying and probing questions.
6. Determining next steps and probing questions.
7. Listing next steps on a T-chart, with the left column titled "What do we want to know more about?" and the right column titled "What can we do?"
8. Reflecting about the debriefing session and determining how to share the conversation, information collected, and next steps with staff.
9. Sharing the conversation, information collected, questions, and next steps with staff.
10. Determining as a staff how to follow through on the next steps.

Individual Teacher Feedback

In some schools, the observing colleagues give individual feedback to teachers. When teachers at Huntingtown High School began participating in walkthroughs several years ago, they were asked not to take observation notes. The administration wanted to assure teachers that the walks had no relation to evaluation. As the teaching staff became more comfortable with peer observations, they began to request feedback from their observing colleagues. In the last several years, teachers have been recording anecdotal descriptions of what they observe, and they provide this feedback. They write notes on slips of paper and either meet with individual teachers observed, place notes in their mailboxes, or send e-mail messages.

I know that being involved as an observer in walkthroughs has impacted the way I think about teaching and learning. However, I think the most far-reaching benefit of these walks schoolwide is when we are interacting with one another in regards to what this data collection reveals.

—Lindsey Yundt, 9th Grade Math Teacher,
South Junior High School, Idaho

Staff at Lancaster High School use the observation protocol developed by UCLA Center X for their Powerlesson walkthroughs. This protocol asks teachers being observed to identify what they want observers to notice. Teachers to be observed meet with the team of observers who, in turn, may ask clarifying questions about the teachers' focus on instruction. The team members use objective language to describe what they see during the walkthroughs. The observed teachers have the opportunity to reflect on the feedback and determine the relevance of the information.

The nature of feedback at Crystal River Elementary School evolved over time. At first, teachers definitely wanted feedback from their peer observers, so note cards were created for that purpose. After a while, teachers wanted to make sure the feedback was balanced, so they included positive and constructive comments. Some teachers felt uncomfortable with constructive feedback coming from their colleagues, so ultimately, the teachers' Interest-Based Bargaining Group decided that only principals and instructional facilitators could give feedback. The school's principal now asks the teachers conducting walkthroughs for input on the feedback to be given to teachers. In an effort to maintain objective, nonjudgmental language, the principal reads her report to the walkthrough team before meeting with the teachers who have been observed.

Other Forms of Feedback

In addition to face-to-face communications, teachers share their walk-through observations in other ways. Fort Vancouver High School uses a monthly instructional newsletter to present walkthrough data to the faculty. This newsletter also keeps faculty current with the latest school improvement initiatives, learning targets, and research in education that could inform a future walkthrough focus.

Teams of teachers at Martin Luther King, Jr. Middle School visit classrooms quarterly for 10 minutes each. The focus of these walkthroughs is based on the professional development in which teachers have participated. After walks are completed, the observing teacher teams summarize the patterns of the focus area and engage in reflective conversations about the data. They turn the information over to the principal, who then consolidates it into a letter to the faculty (see the example in Appendix H, Attachment F). The specific look-fors for that quarterly walkthrough are included, along with evidence that supports the focus area in practice.

At both schools, the observations reported by newsletter or letter serve as valued data that become the subject of subsequent discussions at schoolwide or department-level meetings.

No Feedback

We discovered that at some schools, such as Cheney Middle School, feedback is not given to the teachers observed. Teachers are simply thanked for opening their classrooms to observers. The same is true of Griffith Elementary School, although teachers may choose to request feedback. In both schools, the goal of the walkthroughs is for the observing teachers to compare their own instructional practices with those of the teachers they observed. The real benefits of the walkthroughs are realized when observers meet to discuss and reflect on their observations. The intent is for the observing teachers to identify new or revised teaching practices they want to implement in their own classrooms based on their observations of others.

Follow-up Action Steps

Professional conversations among teachers following walkthroughs are crucial to the development of follow-up plans. It is extremely important to engage staff in identifying ways to support implementation of suggested plans of action. Changes made as a result of examining walkthrough data complete the cycle of improvement. This cycle began with a focus and look-fors and continued by observing classroom practices, analyzing and sharing observation data in follow-up reflection and discussion, and finally, taking action steps indicated by the data and subsequent discussions. The cycle is then repeated as action steps become the new focus.

A result of walkthrough dialogue is to plan professional development based on observation data. One middle school had interactive whiteboards in every classroom, but observers noticed that the boards were not being used as instructional tools. As a result of the walkthrough data, the school focused professional development on the use of interactive whiteboard technology as a tool in lesson planning and delivery. In another high school, teacher observers noticed that in most classrooms, students were doing worksheets or teachers were standing in front of the class conducting question-and-answer reviews of the subject matter. These activities did not look like "best practice" in action, so the professional development team introduced a year-long series of workshops on expanding ways for teachers to actively engage students in their lessons.

Other examples of next action steps we found among schools based on teacher walkthrough data included the following:

- Revision of the school improvement plans and goals.
- Identification of specific situations in which teachers may benefit from instructional coaching.
- Identification of teachers who are masters at specific instructional strategies and could model lessons for others or lead professional development.

- Identification of additional administrative support (such as resources and time) needed to implement a new initiative.
- Promotion of other faculty to participate as walkthrough observers or as the observed.
- Intervisitations of teachers across schools within and outside of the school district.
- Reporting and display of observation data to celebrate successes.
- Direction for the focus of future peer walkthrough observations.

Teachers in some schools make commitments to one another to further positive practices around an instructional or curricular initiative. For example, teachers at Ball Junior High School make commitments to one another to promote the positive trends observed from the walkthroughs. For public display among their colleagues, teachers make their commitment in writing: "I promise to incorporate more _____ in my classroom during the next unit."

> When I experience powerful learning during a learning walk, I will do whatever is necessary to make the strategies connected to that experience part of my own teaching repertoire.
>
> —*Kristin J. Takach, Reading Teacher, Williamsport Area High School*

David Shepard, lead consultant for the education consulting firm The Middle Matters, recommends that schools create an action plan for teachers to guide improvement efforts based on the results of teacher walkthrough observation data. Shepard feels that without some type of accountability follow-up, improvement stemming from the walkthrough process is less likely. Department, subject-level, or grade-level teams can complete the action plan using a template such as the one shown in Figure 3.9, and they can self-monitor commitments by sharing results before and after specific instructional events.

Shepard also recommends the creation of an action plan form such as the one shown in Figure 3.10 for individual teachers' accountability to one another. On this form, teachers indicate specifically what they will implement on a future lesson based on walkthrough observation data. Figure 3.11 illustrates a completed action plan form on which the teacher recorded the area of focus he or she committed to improve over a specified period of time.

FIGURE 3.9
Action Plan Template

Beginning [date] _____ the following teachers/staff _____

_____

will [do what?] _____

_____

[how often?] _____

_____

with [form? statement? report?] _____

_____

being submitted to [whom?] _____ as a measure of commitment.

FIGURE 3.10
Individual Teacher Action Plan

Action Plan #1: Lesson Objective and Agenda

Based upon data compiled by three sets of observations, the staff and leadership have identified the posting of and referring to both the daily objective and daily agenda as a priority. Beginning March 7, all faculty should prominently post and refer to the current objective ("I will learn . . .") and agenda ("I will do . . .") for the day. A goal of three references by the teacher to the daily objective for each period is encouraged.

DIRECTIONS: Mark the number of times each day you were able to exhibit the action below.

I worked on the following:

Lesson/unit topic:

	Posted the objective	Referred to the objective	Posted the agenda	Referred to the agenda
Monday				
Tuesday				
Wednesday				
Thursday				
Friday				

FIGURE 3.11
FIGURE 3.11
Sample of Completed Teacher Action Plan

Action Plan #1: Questioning Structure: Priority set by faculty on September 20

Based upon data compiled from a number of walkthrough observations, the staff and leadership of the school have identified questioning structure as a priority. Beginning October 1, all teachers will consciously work to improve the effectiveness of questioning during instruction.

DIRECTIONS: Mark the number of times each day you were able to exhibit the action below.

I worked on the following:
Strategies for increasing student participation during discussions, raising the number of higher-order questions asked.

Lesson/unit topic:
Guiding students in identifying how language, arts, music, belief systems, and other cultural elements can facilitate global understanding or cause misunderstanding.

Days Oct. 1–5	Providing 4–7 second wait time	Reducing "call-out" answers	Increasing % of responders	Asking higher-order questions	Providing cues and prompts for reluctant responders
Monday	2	6	35%	8	4
Tuesday	6	6	45%	12	8
Wednesday	6	5	65%	11	7
Thursday	7	3	70%	14	12
Friday	6	1	85%	15	11

Lessons Learned and Moving Forward

Whether you select a national walkthrough model or develop one tailored to your school, the components are the same. Those components include the protocol (for example, frequency and length of classroom visits), participants, focus and look-fors, data-gathering process, and follow-up discussion. In creating your own model, there is value in reviewing different walkthrough models and selecting the parts that best meet the needs of your school.

Models we found in different schools vary by which teachers participate as the observers, as well as in the frequency and length of observations. In some cases, teachers walk alone; in other settings, they walk as teams. The frequency of teacher walkthrough opportunities ranges from once a week to once a year, with most occurring four times a year. The length of time generally spent in each classroom is 10 minutes or less.

Participants usually use some type of form to record observations of the teaching and learning occurring in the classrooms. Forms can be a checklist of observable indicators, a checklist with space for written comments, or a form with space for written comments. Increasingly, schools are using various software programs or mobile apps for the collection, storage, and presentation of teacher walkthrough data. Some observation teams provide no feedback, depending on the decision of the school.

Reflective discussions among the observers and the observed are the most frequent form of follow-up to teacher walkthroughs. These discussions often center on the description and analysis of walkthrough observation data that indicate trends of instruction and learning. Such questioning and discussion enable teachers to analyze their existing instructional strategies and practices, develop alternative strategies, and identify priorities for future action.

The continuum of a particular walkthrough ends when action steps for change actually take place. These action steps include determining necessary professional development, identifying the focus for future walkthroughs, establishing coaching arrangements, and individual teachers making commitments to improving their skills and learning practices. The walkthrough process continues.

All walkthrough models featured in this book represent works in progress. These schools recognize that teachers' self-interest and success are inextricably tied to the well-being of their students. These schools recognize and respect the teaching staff as the experts in instructional practice and student performance.

Questions to Think About

- Will you select an existing walkthrough model or develop your own?
- Which model(s) might inform the development of your own model?
- How can teachers be encouraged to open their classrooms for walkthroughs and participate as observers?

- What sources should your school draw upon to identify the focus and look-fors in your walkthroughs?
- What are your school's most immediate areas of focus for walkthrough observations?
- What kind of observation form, software program, or technology will teachers want to use to record and report walkthrough data?
- How will you provide observation follow-up to the teachers?
- How will you determine the next steps to be taken after the completion of walkthroughs so improved teaching and student learning occur as a result?

Our Recommendations

- Involve the entire teaching staff early in the process of the planning, selection/design, and implementation of the walkthrough process.
- Provide multiple opportunities for discussions about the value and implementation of the walkthrough process.
- Review the various models of walkthroughs before selecting or developing one that meets your school's culture, needs, and goals.
- Involve teachers in the identification of the focus areas and look-fors.
- Provide opportunities for all teachers to participate in walkthroughs both as observers and as the observed.
- Explore the use of observation software or mobile apps to ease the process of recording observations through walkthroughs.
- Involve teachers in creating the purposes and format for feedback and follow-up.
- Record all walkthrough observations using objective and nonjudgmental language.
- Link each phase of the development of the walkthroughs process—design and selection, implementation, action for improvement, and evaluation.
- Create actionable next steps after thoroughly examining and discussing walkthrough data.

CHAPTER 4

Strategies for Getting
Teachers Involved

When teachers have an opportunity to observe and interact with their colleagues in a nonevaluative way regarding instruction, everyone wins.

—Robert Marzano

We were interested to learn how the schools we studied achieved teacher buy-in for walkthroughs. Even though schools differed in their approaches to getting teachers involved, we found some similarities in their strategies for introducing and implementing this process. In this chapter, we share the most effective strategies: working with teacher leaders or the school leadership team; having a clear, definable purpose for the walkthroughs; carefully planning and gradually introducing the process; being transparent in all aspects of the walkthroughs; developing norms to guide behaviors during and after the walks; providing training on walkthroughs; arranging and scheduling time for teachers to observe and reflect; beginning with volunteers to participate in walkthroughs; focusing observations on student learning rather than on teachers teaching; and maintaining nonjudgmental reflective conversations following walkthroughs.

Teacher Leaders

Strategy #1: Actively involve individual teacher leaders or the school leadership team—or both—in communicating, advocating, and implementing schoolwide teacher involvement in walkthroughs.

Many schools build advocacy among individual teachers or the school leadership team for introducing walkthroughs to the remainder of the staff. This teacher advocacy is vital to the success of any new initiative. Teachers inform their colleagues about the new initiative and its value. During a staff meeting at Cheney Middle School, several teacher leaders explained the teacher walkthrough process and solicited teacher interest in participating. They stated emphatically that the walkthrough process would be focused on student learning, not teacher performance. They also suggested that walkthroughs gave teacher observers an opportunity to assess their own instruction. To initiate the process, the teacher leaders conducted a survey of the staff that asked two questions: (1) Are you willing to open your classroom for observations? and (2) Do you want to participate in a classroom visit? To their surprise, a significant number of teachers volunteered to open their classrooms and expressed an interest in visiting other classrooms.

> Start your teacher walkthrough process with key people at your site whom teachers respect and trust and who have some influence over other teachers.
>
> —*Diana Fujimoto,*
> *Lesson Design Specialist,*
> *Katella High School*

The school leadership team can also be a powerful and influential advocate for walkthroughs by soliciting faculty commitment and engagement. The team can assume responsibility for maintaining open communication about all aspects of walkthroughs so the process is totally transparent to the entire staff. The team can help with the trust building necessary for the successful implementation of walkthroughs by listening to the faculty, responding to concerns and issues, and continually communicating the progress of the walkthrough process.

Such advocacy by a school leadership team is present at Benton Grade School K–4. Their school leadership team, ASPIRE, wanted to investigate the concept of teachers observing teachers. An independent consultant was brought in to explain what the walkthroughs would entail, the accruing benefits, the fact that they were not to be used for any type of teacher evaluation, and the option that the school had to design its own model. This initial introduction ensured the team's comfort level with walkthroughs and made it easier for them to convince the rest of the staff to engage in the effort. The members of ASPIRE offered to be the first teachers to conduct walks and volunteered their rooms for other teachers to observe.

Another example of building leadership team advocacy is in Roaring Fork School District in Colorado. Here, the superintendent set expectations at the outset for all principals to walk together in one another's buildings in small groups and then take the process into their own buildings. The principals subsequently involved members of their school leadership teams in conducting walks. After thorough training, school leadership team members were able to champion the cause of walkthroughs in their respective schools.

Like many schools across the United States, Katella High School experienced a high rate of administrative turnover (four principals in eight years). It fell to the school leadership team to maintain consistently strong connections and trust with the staff for the continuation of the classroom focus walks despite numerous changes in school administrators.

Clear, Definable Purpose

Strategy #2: Clearly define and communicate the purpose of walkthroughs as an important aspect of continuous school improvement.

Establishing a clear and definable purpose for walkthroughs is the second strategy to consider in your school's approach to continuous improvement. The purpose will ultimately determine whether your school will develop its own walkthrough model or adopt an existing one. The fundamental purpose for walkthroughs at all the schools we studied was to improve student learning through the improvement of instructional practices. However, to achieve that outcome, we found that the focus of walkthroughs varied among schools based on their improvement goals and needs.

Your districtwide and schoolwide improvement goals will guide your walkthrough purpose. Answers to the following questions inform that purpose:

- What outcomes do you expect from your walkthrough process?
- How will your walkthroughs complement other school improvement efforts?
- What actions will result from your walkthroughs and subsequent reflective discussions?
- How will you measure the impact of the walkthroughs on teaching and learning?

Make sure teachers are well-versed in the purpose of walkthroughs and how to conduct them.

—*Kristen Tepper,*
former assistant principal,
Lancaster High School

Figure 4.1 shows the purposes for walkthroughs identified by several schools. These purposes include sharing instructional ideas, practices, and resources related to the implementation of new instructional or curricular initiatives; promoting teacher self-assessment and self-reflection; advocating professional conversations regarding walkthrough data; and examining student learning across the school to identify gaps that need to be addressed in teaching and learning.

It is critical that administrators and teachers work together to develop the purposes of the walkthroughs. Working together ensures a relationship of understanding and trust.

Carefully Planned, Gradual Introduction

Strategy #3: Address the concept of walkthroughs with a great deal of thoughtful planning, and introduce the concept carefully and gradually.

We learned that a third important strategy is to invest the time necessary to plan the walkthrough process carefully and implement it as a deliberately patient, gradual process. Gradual implementation creates trust in the process and conveys the value of the walks. Planning entails a meticulous process involving a series of steps that build up to the actual walkthrough implementation.

FIGURE 4.1
Examples of Teacher Walkthrough Purposes

School	Teacher Walkthrough Purpose(s)
Belleville East and West High Schools (Illinois)	Gather observational data about student-engaged learning in order to arrive at a schoolwide profile about student learning practices that can serve as the basis for faculty study, reflection, and instructional improvement.
Bridges High School (Colorado)	Two purposes: (1) Adjust professional development needs and (2) Measure progress in achieving school goals by combining three sources of data: walkthrough information, progress on school goals as reported weekly by teachers, and quarterly student evaluations.
DeWitt Perry Middle School (Texas)	Two purposes: (1) Acquire a clear picture of what is happening instructionally across the school as related to pre-identified problem of practice; and (2) Give teachers individual feedback about how they are doing on the short-term improvement targets to address the problem of practice.
Fontana Unified School District (California)	Support new teachers by observing exceptional and experienced teachers across the district.
Jonesboro High School (Arkansas)	Improve instruction by familiarizing teachers with research-based instructional strategies and providing opportunities to share best practices among the faculty.
Parkway Elementary School (Connecticut)	Develop a professional learning community in which teachers take responsibility for their own learning and reflect on their teaching, thereby continually improving their instructional practice.
Randels Elementary School (Michigan)	Provide teachers' feedback to one another in order to improve instruction on a specific schoolwide area of improvement (e.g., Board Math Initiative).
Salt Creek Elementary School (California)	Observe, support, and share the implementation of new instructional or curricular school improvement strategies (e.g., state curriculum standards, literacy, higher-order questioning, use of technology, *Classroom Instruction That Works*).
South Junior High School (California)	Acquire a snapshot of what students are doing in the classroom to acquire a first-hand glimpse at how students are reacting to instruction and internalizing the content, as well as to discover where and why any students are struggling.

Featured schools suggested that in planning for walkthroughs, the following steps should be followed:

- Visit other schools to observe how walkthroughs are conducted, or at least hold conversations with those schools about the process.
- Ascertain ways for teachers' concerns, issues, and suggestions to be addressed throughout the process.
- Determine and communicate clear and specific purposes for the walkthroughs.

- Develop protocols for the walkthroughs.
- Decide how the process will be initiated and who will be involved from the beginning.
- Define norms or guidelines to govern the process.
- Identify the purpose of observation data and how that data will be shared.
- Pilot the walkthroughs and determine how you will evaluate the process.

Administrators note that teachers may need time to learn about the walkthrough process, be part of the process, and see how the observation data can be used to improve their own teaching and student learning. Teachers at Bridges High School took time to study, inquire about, debate, clarify, and reach consensus on the walkthrough protocol they eventually implemented. As the concept of teachers observing peers was introduced, the process was kept very simple in terms of what to observe, how to record observation data, and how to share information throughout the school.

The staff at Monitor Elementary School determined that going slowly with the process was important. They wanted to build a very strong foundation for classroom walkthroughs as a professional learning tool, and it was important for everyone in that school to feel comfortable with the process. Monitor also wanted to establish a tradition of professional conversations so that no teacher would feel threatened about what was going to be said by peers after classroom visits.

I would recommend to schools/districts considering any walkthrough process to start with their new teachers. They are new, excited, and more willing, and you can make it part of their new-teacher induction requirements. Once they are on board, you can expand outward.

—*Sue Kind, BTSA Support Provider/ Consulting Teacher, Fontana School District*

At South Junior High School in Idaho, the principal gave teachers an overview of the walkthrough process. The principal felt that the process had to be implemented slowly and carefully as a pilot because it was very different from anything that teachers had experienced before. As a result of the pilot, the school adjusted the walkthrough protocols to ease faculty concerns and win their acceptance.

It took two years at Katella High School for the most reluctant participants to accept a role in walkthroughs. It took patience and teachers sharing the benefits they derived from observing peers. Teachers began to realize this value when they noticed that some of the ideas and strategies observed were beginning to create positive changes in student engagement and achievement. Teachers also realized the need for specific professional development from data derived from classroom learning walks.

Transparent Process

Strategy #4: Ensure that every step of the walkthrough process is completely transparent so everyone knows the purpose, the protocols, and what to expect.

We use the word *transparency* in this book because it is such a critical component. Making the entire process transparent—operating in such a way that everyone can see and understand what is taking place in a school setting and why—is the fourth strategy for introducing walkthroughs. Based on what we learned, we emphatically stress that transparency is vital to the building of trust and buy-in for teacher involvement in walkthroughs. Every educator in your school must know the exact purpose and protocol of walkthroughs so there is no confusion or misunderstanding. *That* is transparency.

According to Lisa Allen, a member of the professional development team at South Junior High School in California,

> We wanted to make the first walkthrough as transparent as possible to the entire staff. Making the process transparent and open to the staff was a large part of building the trust. We explained all parts of the classroom walkthroughs prior to implementation and reported everything that we observed. This idea of using teacher observations in classrooms to drive our work is different from the status quo and can be perceived as scary to many teachers. This is why it is so important to let them know all the details of what is reported and how it is used.

A former assistant principal at Lancaster High School informed us that it is extremely important to explain the purpose of the walkthroughs to staff. Whenever there is discomfort with the process, it is crucial to share the reasons behind the steps and make sure the walkthroughs are meaningful to individual teachers. The administration at Lancaster helped the staff work through uncomfortable feelings that came from doing something so new and different. They worked hard to ensure that the staff knew the entire process before implementation of the walks. In addition, they regularly reminded staff that the intent of the teacher walks was to look at learning, not their peers, and that they were definitely not for teacher evaluation.

> Fear of the unknown is powerful, and we needed to continually communicate a consistent message of the process, the goals, and how the teacher walkthrough data was being used.
>
> —*Karen Olson, Principal,*
> *Crystal River Elementary School*

Teachers need to know that classroom walkthroughs are not a "gotcha" activity. Rather, walkthroughs are opportunities for teachers to learn from one another and help identify practices that might need refinement. Therefore, it is essential that all staff members understand the entire walkthrough protocol that will involve them as both the observer and the observed. For the teacher walkthrough process in your school to be transparent, everyone on staff must understand the following points:

- The purpose of the walkthroughs.
- The focus and look-fors.
- Who will be observing and who will be observed.
- The schedule, frequency, and length of walks.
- What happens to the observation data.
- The format for feedback and follow-up.
- The steps for further refinement of the walkthrough process.

Walkthrough Norms

Strategy #5: Create schoolwide norms for walkthroughs and subsequent professional conversations.

Teachers are included as walkthrough observers so they can acquire a wide range of instructional ideas, practices, and resources—not for the purpose of judging or evaluating one another's teaching. To help with this effort, a set of operating norms for walkthroughs must be developed. These norms convey expected behaviors during the actual walks and encourage interdependence and positive sharing among teachers from the walkthrough experiences. Norms specify those actions that are proper and those that are inappropriate. We strongly recommend that administrators and teachers develop walkthrough norms collaboratively. The norms should be reviewed periodically by staff, revised and adjusted as necessary, and followed consistently by all participants in all walkthroughs.

During the Walks

Walkthrough norms from several schools provide useful examples. Here are the walking norms expected of teachers observing classrooms at Fort Vancouver High School:

- Sit or stand quietly in an unobtrusive place, such as at the back of the room or in an empty chair.
- Refrain from redirecting student work or behavior (except in emergency situations) during the learning walk.
- Have a nonevaluative state of mind. Stay focused on gathering data about student learning that you see or elements of instruction that facilitate student learning.
- Use open, nonjudgmental body language.
- If asked a question by a student during your observation, reflect the question back to the student in order to encourage continued learning.

- Ask students about their learning if it is appropriate and can be done without interrupting instruction or learning.

Here are the norms expected of walkthrough participants at Leonard J. Tyl Middle School:

- Set a focus question before the walk, and let the classroom teachers know what that question is before the walking day.
- Do not enter classrooms during the first or last five minutes of class.
- Observe students for five minutes per classroom.
- Leave clipboards and other materials outside of the classroom.
- Interact with students only if they are working in groups, not during whole-class instruction.
- Do not interfere with instruction.
- Observe students using the focus question only.
- Most important, note only what you see—not what you don't see.
- Take notes after the classroom visit and discuss briefly in the hallway as needed.
- Meet at a preplanned time to debrief and invite all faculty members to observe the debriefing session. Only walking teachers may contribute to the debriefing session.

The teachers doing walkthroughs at James Hubert Blake High School follow these norms:

- Write down exact quotes instead of paraphrasing a teacher or student.
- Refrain from talking about the classes you visit until the debriefing.
- Use eye contact with the rest of your group to determine when it is time to leave each class.
- You may talk quietly with a student if the lesson allows it; you can ask something about the category for which you are looking; or you could ask what happened in the lesson before you arrived or about some other relevant topic.

Here are additional examples of walkthrough norms or ground rules found in other schools:

- Turn off cell phones.

- Use agreed-upon common language for describing high-quality instruction.
- Maintain fidelity to the walkthrough protocol.
- Do not speak to one another while in the classroom.
- Observe the classroom from the perspective of the student as a learner.
- Do not teach or assist individuals or small groups with assigned seatwork.
- Depart the classroom when the timekeeper signals that it is time to leave.
- Exit the classroom quietly and expeditiously.

After the Walks

We recommend that school staffs develop norms to establish guidelines for conversations that follow walkthrough observations. The teachers at Cheney Middle School identified what they termed "group operating principles" to govern discussions when sharing walkthrough data. These principles include the following:

- Listen to, welcome, and consider others' ideas.
- Encourage every voice.
- Accept and honor each person.
- Create opportunities for and value humor and fun.
- Support emotional collegiality.
- Honor the idea that we are all here to learn and grow together.
- Avoid evaluative language and critique.

The UCLA Center X Classroom Walk-Through, a model used by several of the schools we studied, has the following guidelines for sharing observations:

- Make comments straightforward and clear.
- Ask genuine questions that reflect what you wonder about.
- Avoid leading or multiple-choice questions.
- Do not set up the answer.
- Be clear about your intent: clarifying questions are for the person asking them (*who, what, when, where*), and open-ended probing questions are for the person answering them (*why*).

A few schools established expectations for teacher behavior after the completion of the walkthroughs and follow-up conversations. The teachers at Monitor Elementary School follow several confidentiality rules, which they review at each debriefing session. Observers do not share

- What they have observed in a lesson with anyone outside of the immediate group of observers.
- Comments made during the debriefing with people outside of the debriefing group.
- Suggestions to the observed teacher, unless that teacher explicitly asks for feedback from the walkthrough.

Other examples of norms to govern conversations after walks include the following:

- Challenge ideas, not people.
- Listen to the perspectives of all.
- Encourage the exchange of ideas.
- Ask for clarification if you do not understand what you observed.
- Look for positive ideas you can take away.
- Speak consistently to the observed focus and look-fors.
- Do not ridicule or discount what others observe.
- Seek to build common understanding of language.
- Demonstrate respect for one another and for mutual learning.
- Keep the focus of your comments on what was observed and on the specific area the school wants to improve.
- Engage in deep questioning and conversation to inspire one another.
- Be specific with feedback and comments, with reference to events noted.
- Ask "what if" or "I wondered" reflective questions.
- Keep student learning the central focus of all comments.

Walkthrough Training

Strategy #6: Train teachers on a given walkthrough model that increases their awareness and understanding of the process and its value for improving teaching and learning.

The sixth strategy is to provide training in observations and follow-up reflective discussions. Such training includes how to observe classroom behaviors, familiarity with the focus and look-fors and accompanying obser-vation forms or software, how to remain nonjudgmental in recording data, and how to summarize and discuss trends in practices without being judgmental.

For those schools using a nationally or regionally known walkthrough model (see Figure 3.2 on pages 36–40), training is built into the process. This training typically prepares participants to conduct observations effectively in short periods of time and to hold collegial, reflective follow-up discussions. In some cases, participants practice observing by viewing demonstrations or vid-eotapes of instruction. For the schools that use the UCLA Center X Classroom Walk-Through, an initial five-day training introduces participants to the vari-ous elements of the protocol, including how to (1) create effective focus ques-tions to guide observations; (2) collect and record observed evidence; (3) determine patterns and trends in the data; (4) raise questions for inquiry; and (5) plan the next steps based on the inquiry questions.

Walkthrough observers for the Data-in-a-Day model at Cleveland High School watched a 20-minute teaching simulation as part of their walkthrough preparation. This training increased observing team members' comfort as contributors, and it improved the inter-rater reliability of their observations. Following the teaching simulation, observers compared their observation notes, clarified their perspectives, and perfected their focus on exactly what should be observed.

> Get the right people in place, have them trained, and give them an opportunity to experi-ence and practice with the classroom walkthrough pro-cess.
>
> *—Shannon Hoos, Lesson Design Specialist,*
> *Ball Junior High School*

Educators in Belleville Township High School District 201 are required to be trained in using the Instructional Practices Inventory, a process for profil-ing student-engaged learning. The training is designed to ensure that teacher observers become accurate data collectors. It also provides them with strategies for using data as the basis for collaborative data-analysis conversations and subsequent problem solving and goal setting by the teaching staff.

The teacher walkthrough process at Roaring Fork School District began with training for a districtwide leadership team (superintendent, principals, and instructional facilitators) and two teachers from each school. They received training from McREL on how to use their Power Walkthrough System and observation templates (which the district could modify to meet its own purposes). They learned how to use nonjudgmental language for their observations and how to engage in conversations with students about what they were learning.

> Teachers doing the walk-throughs do not give any feedback to the staff at any time, even if they ask. This is hard for observers as they want to praise the staff and tell them they are doing a great job. No judgment statements are made, either positive or negative. We just want to share descriptive patterns of instruction for whole-school reflective discussions.
>
> —*Betty Olson, Principal,*
> *South Junior High School, Idaho*

Administrators and lead teachers at the 17 schools of Talladega Public Schools attended training on the Instructional Rounds Network (City et al., 2009), which was provided by the Alabama Best Practices Center. The Instructional Rounds training convinced these administrators and teachers that the model would provide real-time data on instruction and enable them to make instructional and curricular adjustments quickly. Furthermore, the model provided an avenue for educators across the entire school district to work together more closely to improve student achievement.

The principal at South Junior High School in Idaho attended the Look 2 Learning (L2L) Training and Engagement Conference in October 2008. She appreciated this walkthrough model because it is nonevaluative, teachers are actively involved throughout the process, and the whole staff uses the data to make decisions for staff development. She became a certified L2L trainer, allowing her to return to her school and introduce and train her staff in the L2L walkthrough protocol. She presented an overview and proposal to her district administration to pilot the program at her school and to train teacher leaders at five other district schools. Today, the L2L walks occur districtwide and are part of the district's strategic plan.

Even when schools develop their own walkthrough protocols, the process includes efforts to prepare the teachers for observing one another. For example, the teachers at Fort Vancouver High School use staff meetings to practice using a rubric for walkthrough observations and discuss their observations collectively by watching videos of teaching. The practice sessions are also a way to test the usefulness of the rubric to guide observations.

At Huntingtown High School, teachers viewed Internet video clips of classroom instruction as part of their observation training. The videos, some of which showed actual Huntingtown teachers in their own classrooms, were used to familiarize teachers with the checklist designed for walkthrough observations and to help them practice focusing on what to observe.

Scheduling Walkthroughs and Follow-up Time

Strategy #7: Prepare a schedule that gives teachers time for walkthrough observations and subsequent professional conversations.

Although many teachers realize the value of walkthroughs, a major challenge mentioned repeatedly was time—how to find the time in teachers' schedules to do classroom walks and conduct reflective discussions about the observations afterwards. The schools in this book shared a number of ways to carve time out of the school day for observations and conversations.

At Monitor Elementary School, every grade level has a protected 45-minute period, once a week, that is used for walkthroughs. The first 30 minutes are for the walkthroughs; the remaining 15 minutes are for reflective conversations.

Leaders at Parkway Elementary School demonstrate their commitment to walkthroughs early in the year. Specific dates and blocks of time are placed on the school calendar to ensure that walkthroughs occur. Teachers have the opportunity to sign up for times to participate in those walkthroughs both as observers and as hosts. Whole-school debriefing sessions are held during before-school meetings or are part of regularly scheduled staff meetings.

Ball Junior High School schedules daylong walkthroughs three times a year. Two teachers who serve as walkthrough facilitators have substitute teachers for the day so each can join a walking team. Their participation helps ensure that walkthrough protocols are followed. The majority of Ball's teachers participate in the walks during their planning periods. The follow-up discussions occur one or two days after the walks, during the school's scheduled staff-development time.

South Junior High School in California uses "early-release Thursdays" for walkthrough follow-up discussion. The school designated these days for other professional development, but now South's staff members use them to discuss their walkthrough data and plan follow-up action steps based on the data.

The administration and teaching staff at Lancaster High School use teacher planning time, staff meetings, and department meetings for the walkthrough process. They are even able to use categorical funds to pay teachers who participate in the debriefing sessions after school.

The Burlington High School administration gives teachers structured time to participate in walkthroughs and collaborate in follow-up discussions. The structured time frees teachers from some of the duties related to their prep and duty periods.

Here is a summary of ways to provide time for teachers to participate in walkthroughs and follow-up discussions:

- Hire floating substitute teachers to cover classes of observing teachers.
- Use the principal, assistant principal, instructional coaches, mentors, or aides to cover classes of those teachers participating in walks.
- Combine classes, if teachers agree, so teachers can be released to participate in walkthroughs.
- Seek approval to use department-, subject-, or grade-level common planning time for debriefings.
- Use school staff meetings and department-level meetings to share observations and conduct reflective conversations.
- Use late-start or early-release staff development days for follow-up meetings and discussions.
- Use individual teacher planning time when no other options are available and if teachers agree.

Despite the challenges of finding walkthrough time for teachers, the schools we studied are committed to the successful implementation of walkthroughs. Providing time for teachers to observe one another and discuss those observations is a part of comprehensive school improvement efforts. Each school addressed these challenges in the most creative way it could find.

Beginning with Volunteers

Strategy #8: Encourage teachers to volunteer as participants in the teacher walkthrough process.

An eighth strategy to involve teachers in the walkthrough process is to begin the process with volunteers—as both observers and observed. Finding volunteers willing to investigate and participate in a new building initiative often leads to a smoother implementation. Volunteers who find the experience beneficial are willing and excited to share the benefits and encourage other faculty to participate.

Sandra Sweeten, a member of the professional development team at South Junior High School in California, shares this recollection:

> We started out with only volunteers and slowly added participants. This is not a process that should be forced on the staff. This allowed those volunteering teachers to share their observations and experience of the process with others. They were focusing on the students, and this gave them the chance to see what's working and what can make instruction more effective. All of the patterns and trends of their observations were taken to our staff debriefing meetings so that everyone could see what was being written. They were very careful to make sure that nothing was evaluative or specific enough to trace back to content. It was important to the volunteers that everyone saw that this was a nonthreatening process. Their experiences helped build a base of advocacy that grew over time, helped others to trust the process, and slowly built a school culture that uses the experience of our students to drive curriculum improvement.

ASPIRE, the school leadership team at Benton Grade School K–4, introduced the concept of walkthroughs by asking teachers to volunteer for walkthroughs *without* students in the classrooms. Jeff Nelsen of Targeted Learning Walks calls these "ghost walks." According to Nelsen, ghost walks include an organized tour of the building by teams of teachers without the presence of students or supervisors. Teams visit peers' classrooms to review student work, portfolios, wall displays, instructional materials, classroom layout, display content, and teacher lesson plans that include scope and sequencing of instruction. Teachers whose rooms are being observed choose the materials to display. ASPIRE invited volunteers to open their classrooms for an after-school walk to display their work on a schoolwide reading initiative. In turn, the entire teaching staff was invited to volunteer for walking in peers' classrooms. Many teacher participants recorded and photographed ideas from other classrooms to implement in their own.

Teachers at E. R. Geddes Elementary School are given a choice to open their rooms for visitation by other teachers as part of the walkthrough process. Teachers are not required to become observers or to open their classrooms for observations. Nevertheless, the number of teachers who participate continues to grow year after year.

Focusing on Student Learning

Strategy #9: Make student learning, rather than teachers teaching, the primary target of observations during walkthroughs.

Some classroom walkthroughs focus strictly on student learning. This is an effective strategy for introducing walkthroughs as it may help ease teachers' anxieties. Instead of focusing on teacher behavior, observers watch and interact with students to determine what they know and can do as a result of instruction. These observations can provide a better picture of how effective instructional practices result in increased student learning. Collecting information about student engagement helps guide a school's identification and implementation of strategies that improve student learning. Walkthroughs provide data, in addition to that collected through formative assessments and standardized tests, to measure students' understanding of what they have learned.

As we've mentioned before, a number of schools use the student-centered UCLA Center X Classroom Walk-Through for observations. Lancaster High School is one example. The teachers at Lancaster created the following focus question for one of their classroom walkthroughs: "What evidence do we see that students are engaged in the process of challenging learning?" By focusing only on students' actions and words, they observed and recorded what students were doing, discussing, and producing in the classroom. This focus provided a schoolwide view of student engagement. In acquiring walkthrough data on this focus question, the staff and students explored indicators of rigorous learning and redefined their work and roles within their learning community.

Another walkthrough model that emphasizes students as the central focus of observations is the Instructional Practices Inventory process. This model, which is used at the Belleville East and West High Schools, is a way to profile student engagement systematically during a specified time frame, typically one school day, so faculty can study and interpret the data to determine future classroom instruction. Observation data are given to the school as a whole so that no teacher, department, or grade level is singled out. Focusing on students and removing any threat of teacher evaluation from the process allows teachers to accept this walkthrough strategy easily.

The staff at Martin Luther King, Jr. Middle School use the Learning Walk Routine. Observers visit classrooms and ask students questions about their learning. They record what students tell them and what they see. Upon completion of the walk, the teams use descriptive, objective language to summarize their observations. They also provide the faculty with a series of thought-provoking questions and ideas that are based on those observations. These walks help teachers assess the school's progress with students on the chosen initiative—not on the performance of any individual teacher. Opportunities such as classroom walkthroughs allow teachers to share what they know about how students learn best. (See Appendix H for a detailed account of the walkthroughs at Martin Luther King, Jr. Middle School.)

When I walk into a classroom, I spend only a split-second observing the teacher before analyzing the level of engagement of each student. I immediately reflect on my own teaching and ask, "If I were teaching this lesson, what would I do to ensure every student was engaged at the highest level possible?"

—*Tammy Butler, Literacy Specialist, Monitor Elementary School*

South Junior High School in Idaho and Burlington High School use the Look 2 Learning walkthrough model. In the L2L model, observers watch students and interact with them about what they are learning. During these walks, observers look for three things: clarity of the lesson objective to students; level of students' critical thinking based on Bloom's taxonomy; and levels of student engagement. The goal of L2L, like the other models mentioned, is to provide all staff with schoolwide data on student learning trends and patterns.

In each of these walkthrough models, students were the primary focus of the observations. This focus illustrates the school staff's commitment to student learning. The observations were free from judgment or evaluation by teachers, and feedback provided data to make ongoing, solid decisions on improving student performance. Furthermore, students benefit from these walkthroughs when they

- See teachers throughout the school working together to refine instruction to meet students' needs.
- See teachers discovering connections among curriculum areas.
- Notice adults throughout the school taking an interest in what and how well they are learning.
- Have opportunities to articulate to visitors what, why, and how they are learning.

Nonjudgmental Conversations Following Walkthroughs

Strategy #10: Share and discuss observation data without any evaluative or judgmental comments.

A tenth and extremely important strategy identified by all of the schools we studied was the effort to engage teachers in reflective discussions about walkthrough data without becoming evaluative or judgmental of others. A serious risk to the successful implementation of walkthroughs is the vulnerability of teachers to criticism by their peers. We know that certain behaviors—recording walkthrough observations; asking reflective questions; and giving feedback in ways that create trust, are nonjudgmental, and encourage a variety of perspectives—do not just happen naturally. Nevertheless, we found schools that were able to keep the process free from judgment or evaluation. Many schools forbade evaluative statements and allowed for no identification of teachers or room numbers during the debriefing of observations.

We located some schools that use trained facilitators to keep the conversations among teachers focused but not evaluative. Cheney Middle School uses a facilitator to guide the follow-up discussions. The school established norms reinforcing the point that the focus of walkthrough observations and conversations remained on student learning and not on teacher performance. During the debriefing, if observers use evaluative language concerning teacher performance, the facilitator redirects the conversation back to student learning.

Some schools created norms for teachers to govern their own offering and receiving of feedback so that productive learning conversations could occur. The staff at Jonesboro High School agreed to norms for walkthroughs, prohibiting the use of evaluative or judgmental language in recording and discussing observations. Before each walk, the observing team reviews those rules.

Other schools provided teacher training in conducting reflective conversations. This training built the capacity of teachers to develop habits and skills in sharing and assessing their own practices, strategies, and expertise. The training includes how to develop a protocol for guiding professional learning conversations; how to establish ground rules that describe nonjudgmental ways to give and receive feedback for productive learning conversations; and how to pose reflective questions to engage the thinking of others. Teachers at South Junior High School in California were introduced to protocols for professional conversations from the Critical Friends Group before the implementation of classroom walkthroughs. Teachers use the protocols for discussing student work, assessments, and teaching dilemmas.

> Our goal is to have teacher observers act as a video camera, recording only what they see or hear. While we try to remain objective and factual, we also review our observations in mini debriefs after each classroom visit. During this time we try to help each other reword our observations so that the evaluative language is taken out.
>
> —*Deb Oda,*
> *Professional Development Coordinator,*
> *South Junior High School, California*

These protocols increase trust and enhance communication, whereby teachers can use data from the classroom walkthroughs to discuss the improvement of student achievement objectively, without fear of criticism.

We strongly recommend providing training for all staff who participate in walkthroughs to ensure that walkthrough data are described objectively. So much of a teacher's day involves evaluating the progress of students that it is a natural part of teacher performance to think of behavior as relatively "good" or "bad." Be forewarned: the use of evaluative language will derail even the best-intentioned walkthrough efforts.

Lessons Learned and Moving Forward

It is one thing to describe what schools do to involve teachers in walkthrough observations and another thing to motivate teachers to accept walkthroughs as beneficial to teaching and learning. The 10 strategies presented in this chapter were developed by schools that successfully gained teacher buy-in for walkthroughs. Here is a review of the strategies:

1. **Actively involve individual teacher leaders or the school leadership team—or both—in communicating, advocating, and implementing schoolwide teacher involvement in walkthroughs.** The role of these teacher leaders is to help inform, educate, and inspire their colleagues to become involved in the walkthrough process.

2. **Clearly define and communicate the purpose of walkthroughs as an important aspect of continuous school improvement.** The purpose will help decide whether it will be preferable to develop a unique walkthrough model or select an existing model.

3. **Address the concept of walkthroughs with a great deal of thoughtful planning, and introduce the concept carefully and gradually.** This helps contribute to building trust among the faculty in the process, participants, and ultimate value of the walks.

4. **Ensure that every step of the walkthrough process is completely transparent so everyone knows the purpose, the protocols, and what to expect.** Trust and buy-in to such walkthroughs are increased if all teachers understand every aspect of the process, from inception to evaluation.

5. **Create schoolwide norms for walkthroughs and subsequent professional conversations.** The norms will contribute to the building of trust among staff in the walkthrough process and encourage the positive sharing of the walkthrough experience among teachers.

6. **Train teachers on a given walkthrough model that increases their awareness and understanding of the process and its value for improving teaching and learning.** Involve them in formal or informal training in observing, recording data in a nonjudgmental way, and conducting descriptive, nonevaluative conversations.

7. **Prepare a schedule that gives teachers time for walkthrough observations and subsequent reflective discussions.** Schools use a variety of ways to accomplish this, such as (a) using substitute teachers, administrators, or other certified personnel within the school to cover classes; (b) seeking teachers' agreement to use their free or planning periods; (c) using whole-school staff and department-, subject-, or grade-level team meeting times; (d) using blocks of time on early-release and late-start days; or (e) occasionally having one teacher monitor two classrooms.

8. **Encourage teachers to volunteer as participants in the teacher walkthrough process.** This strategy begins the process of building trust, works out the issues in the early implementation of walkthroughs, and allows volunteers to influence involvement of their peers in the walks.

9. **Make student learning, rather than teachers teaching, the primary target of observations during walkthroughs.** Along with easing some of the fears and concerns that teachers may have when being observed, the focus on students provides useful schoolwide information on how well they understand and can use the knowledge and skills being taught.

10. **Share and discuss observation data without any evaluative or judgmental comments.** The real objective is to allow promising practices, ideas, and resources from the walkthroughs to be shared among the staff in order to improve schoolwide instruction and student learning.

Questions to Think About

- What are some purposes to consider for your school's walkthroughs?
- How could walkthroughs be introduced to staff members?
- How can the intent and protocols be made transparent to all staff?
- What kind of training will be provided to increase observation and reflective conversation skills?
- How often will the walkthroughs be conducted, and how long will observers typically be in a classroom?
- What arrangements have to be made to schedule time for teachers to conduct walkthroughs and hold reflective discussions?
- How will teachers gather walkthrough data from their observations?
- What kind of follow-up will occur?

Our Recommendations

- Align the purposes of the walkthroughs to districtwide or schoolwide improvement goals.
- Provide training for all teachers on how to be nonevaluative and nonjudgmental in observing, recording, and discussing walkthrough data.
- Build advocacy for walkthroughs by first engaging teacher leaders or the school leadership team, or both, in the planning and early implementation of the process.
- Engage teachers in the development of norms that will guide the behaviors of the teachers in the walkthrough observations and subsequent feedback and follow-up.
- Include newly hired teachers in walkthroughs as a natural part of their teaching and learning experience.
- Open the walkthrough process to volunteers both as the observers and as those willing to open their classrooms for observations.

- Focus teacher observations on student learning rather than on teachers teaching.
- Consider implementing walkthroughs in stages (for example, observations without taking notes; teachers just visiting within their same grade, subject, or department level; teachers volunteering to walk or open their classroom for visits).
- Pilot and practice the walkthrough protocol to assess what is working and what is not working.
- Explore various time schedules and strategies to release teachers from classroom duties in order to observe others and be involved in walkthrough debriefs, reflective discussions, and sharing sessions with other faculty.
- Use data to describe patterns and trends of practices observed, not to evaluate or judge teachers.

CHAPTER 5

Additional Issues to Address

Most teachers are not trained to help peers grow professionally, and the vast majority of teachers find this new role uncomfortable at first.

—Thomas R. Hoerr

The act of peers observing peers in classroom walkthroughs represents quite a shift in a school culture where teachers have taught largely in isolation from one another. It takes time to build trust and confidence in this endeavor until teachers realize the inherent value for themselves and their students. We cannot overemphasize the importance of the planning phase for the entire protocol. This planning ensures continuous monitoring—evaluating and revising the protocol as it is implemented. Aside from the creation and communication of the walkthrough protocols, additional issues need to be addressed during planning for the walks to be successful. In this chapter, we discuss approaching teachers who are reluctant or resistant to participating in walkthroughs; dealing with teacher union concerns; coordinating and tracking the walkthrough process; announcing walkthroughs to staff; connecting walkthroughs to other school improvement efforts; evaluating the walkthrough process; and measuring the impact of walkthroughs on instruction and learning.

Engaging Resistant and Reluctant Teachers

Regardless of the promise a new initiative might bring, research indicates that most educators resist change to some degree (Hall & Hord, 2001). This is certainly true of teacher participation in walkthroughs either as observers or as those being observed. For some teachers, having colleagues come into their classrooms can create anxiety, and the idea of going into another teacher's classroom to observe can feel uncomfortable or even threatening. Teachers may feel insecure regarding their performance; they may feel they will be judged by their peers; they may view the walkthrough process as "just one more thing on a full plate"; and they may resent the interruption of instructional or planning time. Recognizing that there may be some degree of resistance or reluctance to participate, it is imperative to include teachers in the earliest discussions about walkthroughs. After there is some degree of understanding about walkthroughs, you may survey teachers anonymously to gather their thoughts and concerns. Two questions to ask are

- What concerns do you have about classroom walkthroughs?
- What needs to happen in our school for classroom walkthroughs to be an effective professional growth experience?

The first question will bring up issues teachers may hesitate to express openly in a group setting. The second question is stated in a positive way to help establish steps toward developing the protocol. The aim of both questions is to convey that the teacher walkthrough initiative is being strongly considered and will only be successful with teacher understanding, input, and support. This transparent process invites the opinions—even dissenting ones—of all who will be affected by walkthroughs. Sharing the results of this informal survey publicly with the whole staff helps prevent individuals or small groups from sabotaging the initiative.

According to Bergmann and Brough (2007), there are four strategic areas for assisting those most resistant or reluctant to change: motivation, inclusion, communication, and evaluation. These are the same strategic areas we recommend you focus on when planning, implementing, and evaluating classroom walkthroughs. The schools we studied shared the following recommendations for addressing teacher reluctance or resistance to walkthroughs in those four essential strategic areas.

Motivation

- Keep walkthroughs focused on student learning rather than on teachers.
- Ask teacher leaders to contact and encourage all teachers to participate in the walkthrough process.
- Demonstrate the value of walkthroughs in contributing to the school's collaborative culture.
- Celebrate all teachers as they show interest in walkthroughs and begin to participate in them.
- Invite resistant or reluctant teachers to participate in walkthroughs at a school where the process is working successfully, and have them talk to teachers involved.

Inclusion

- Ensure that all teachers are involved in the walkthrough process from the very beginning—initial conversations, training, and implementation—to help break down resistance.
- Provide opportunities for all teachers to express their concerns and suggestions in a safe environment.
- Invite resistant teachers to participate in the development of the walking norms for the walkthrough protocol and follow-up conversations.
- Ask resistant or reluctant teachers to walk with their peers to observe the process in action.
- Practice patience, recognizing that change takes time.

Communication

- Be completely transparent throughout the process—introducing, planning, and implementing walkthroughs.
- Assure teachers continuously that walkthroughs are not any part of their performance evaluation.
- Use time in staff meetings for teachers to share their walkthrough experiences.
- Continually communicate with all staff members on the progress of walkthroughs and how they are impacting school improvement.

Evaluation

- Use teacher input to ensure that the walkthroughs align with other school improvement goals.
- Seek involvement of all teachers in evaluating the walkthrough process, continually striving for improvement.
- Involve all teachers in developing measures for determining the impact of walkthroughs on teaching and learning.

Although not all teachers will be enthusiastic about walkthroughs at first, they are more likely to accept the process when they have been approached for their thoughts and suggestions. The real challenge, according to the principal at Mohegan Elementary School, is to implement a walkthrough process from which the value to the teachers far outweighs all of the downside concerns and risks.

Addressing Teacher Union Issues

Teacher involvement in classroom walkthroughs has not been a major issue with teacher unions in our featured schools for several reasons. First, in many schools, the teachers had ownership of the walkthrough process by being directly involved in the planning and related training. Second, in most schools, teachers were not required to participate but volunteered as observers or by opening their classrooms to observers. Third, none of the schools featured in our study used walkthrough data for teacher evaluation. In fact, most of them took extraordinary steps to reassure teachers that no performance evaluation or judgments about others would be part of walkthroughs.

Three schools noted that there were some teacher union issues with walkthroughs. These included whether any type of teacher evaluation would occur; use of planning time for the walkthrough process; teachers giving feedback to colleagues; number of observers in a classroom at one time; and teachers being required to participate in the walkthroughs.

Bringing in teacher union representatives at the very beginning of walkthrough conversations at Belleville East and West High Schools helped ease concerns about any evaluation connected with walkthroughs. The union representatives were trained with the rest of the staff in the Instructional Practices Inventory model selected for walkthroughs. They learned firsthand that the process focused on student engagement rather than instruction and it was not evaluative of the teacher. Because of their involvement, they realized the intent and benefits of classroom walkthroughs and supported the initiative.

We have come from an era of closed-door teaching to one that is very open indeed, and not all have walked willingly into this new era.

—*Karen Olson, Principal,*
Crystal River Elementary School

Teachers at South Junior High School in Idaho also initially expressed concern that walkthroughs would be used for teacher evaluation. This reaction happened because the top portion of the observation form included space for a teacher's name. Their concern was taken seriously, and the form was revised so that space for names was removed and only the grade level, department, or subject observed was noted, for the purpose of disaggregating the data. Teachers were also reluctant to use their planning time for the walkthrough process, so administrators hired substitute teachers to release teachers from their classroom duties and to allow staff to attend meetings for the follow-up discussions.

The topic of walkthroughs came up at the Roaring Fork School District through their Interest-Based Bargaining (IBB), a collaborative process used by the district to discuss salaries, policies, and workplace issues. The issues about walkthroughs were (1) observers being uncomfortable giving feedback to their peers; (2) the number of observers in classrooms over a day as teams of administrators and teachers spent the majority of a day in the process; and (3) the requirement that teachers participate in walkthroughs. The third concern was immediately dispelled because participation was voluntary. Because teachers felt uncomfortable giving feedback to their colleagues, all participants agreed that feedback would come only from the principal. To ensure clarity of the walkthrough process and its implementation, the IBB created a document that lists the protocols, communication procedures, and alignment of responsibilities of administrators, teachers, instructional facilitators, and the substitute teacher coordinator (see Figure 5.1).

FIGURE 5.1
Walkthrough Agreement

District Purpose

- The main goal of walkthroughs is to improve student outcomes; we know that teachers who consistently teach well are the greatest assets to student learning.
- Ongoing walkthroughs provide a large set of data used to inform the district and schools of the need for further professional development and to support successful delivery of instruction. Follow-up coaching is intended to improve instruction and student outcomes.
- Walkthroughs create a common approach for the delivery of instruction, as well as a common language for discussing instruction. Common language is based on *Classroom Instruction That Works* (CITW), a collection of research-based instructional strategies.
- Walkthroughs are formative assessments providing data to guide future professional development and implementation of CITW. For example, district data identified that setting objectives needed to be implemented more rigorously across all three communities. Since creating and focusing on this goal, data indicate we have improved our practice of setting objectives.

Individual Purpose

- Teachers are included on walkthroughs to help spiral CITW strategies throughout their instruction versus receiving "one-shot" professional development.
- Walkthroughs provide an opportunity for teachers to learn from one another, coming away from classrooms with ideas to try.
- Group discussion provides an opportunity for teachers to see instruction from the perspective of the learners, i.e., what is working and what might benefit from adjusting.
- Feedback is intended to promote self-reflection on the delivery of instruction.

continued

FIGURE 5.1
Walkthrough Agreement (*continued*)

District Protocol

- Walkthroughs will be as unobtrusive as possible.
- Walkthroughs will range from three to five minutes.
- At no point should a walkthrough observation become a component of evaluation.
- When a team is composed of more than four people, prior notice will be given to the affected teacher.
- A teacher's instructional plan should not change or be interrupted during a walkthrough.
- Only administrators and instructional facilitators provide feedback to classroom teachers.
- Walkthroughs should be equitable.
- Teachers are not required to observe a substitute.
- Substitute-teacher data will be disaggregated to provide feedback training for the substitute-teacher bank.
- Substitute-teacher data will not impact classroom teacher data but will be analyzed at school and district levels as its own category.
- Long-term substitutes may be given walkthrough feedback from administrators or instructional facilitators to support their instructional practices.

Communication about Purpose and Protocol

Administrators . . .

- Review purpose and protocol at an administrators' meeting.
- Review purpose and protocol at a staff meeting. Include a handout for all teachers to reference.
- Clarify that walkthrough data are not part of the formal evaluation but an opportunity to observe and gather data regarding learning and implementation of CITW.

Teachers . . .

- Ensure students are aware of walkthrough purpose and protocol.
- Ensure students are informed of their role during walkthroughs.

Instructional Facilitators . . .

- Include information about walkthrough purpose and protocol in induction materials for new teachers.

Substitute Teacher Coordinators . . .

- Reiterate the importance of following teacher lesson plans as written.
- Review purpose and protocol at the beginning-of-the-year substitute teachers' meeting.
- Review purpose and protocol of walkthrough at a staff meeting. Include a handout for all substitute teachers to reference.
- Clarify that walkthrough data are not part of a substitute's formal evaluation but an opportunity to observe and gather data regarding learning and implementation of CITW.

Source: Used with permission from Roaring Fork School District, Carbondale, Colorado.

Coordinating the Walkthrough Process

Including teachers as observers in walkthroughs will create some administrative issues in terms of coordinating and monitoring the process. We found numerous examples of either a principal or an assistant principal who assumed the major responsibility for coordination. In some schools, the principal designated others to take the lead in coordinating the walkthrough process; in other cases, coordination was handled by a special committee on walkthroughs that provided oversight to the process.

Walkthrough coordination was typically delegated to an instructional coach, an instructional strategist, a lead teacher, a resource teacher, or a staff development teacher. At Cheney Middle School, several teacher leaders handle coordination; at Martin Luther King, Jr. Middle School, a lead teacher assumes coordination responsibility; and at Ball Junior High School, it is a lesson-design coach, Title 1 coordinator, and one other teacher leader who coordinate the process. At South Junior High School in Idaho, a teacher helps schedule the walks, ensures that everyone participates, and rotates those who are walking.

In some cases, specially designated walkthrough teams of teachers coordinate the process. At South Junior High School in Idaho, members of the Look 2 Learning Team are in charge of scheduling the walks, processing the walkthrough data, and scheduling team meetings. The Instructional Practices Inventory Data Team led by a teacher leader at Belleville East High School coordinates that school's schedule for the data collectors and summarizes the data from the walkthroughs for presentation to the faculty. At Dr. Charles E. Murphy Elementary School, members of the Professional Learning Visits Team set the dates for the walkthroughs.

We found a broad range of responsibilities associated with coordinating and monitoring walkthroughs. The coordination responsibilities in featured schools included one or more of the following:

- Provide or arrange for training of teachers in walkthroughs (covering such things as protocols, observations, and professional conversations).
- Prepare and communicate the visitation schedule of teachers who will be observing on the walks.
- Communicate with teachers to be observed to ensure clarity of the protocol.
- Help facilitate the creation of the focus question and identification of the look-fors.
- Establish roles and responsibilities of observing team members.
- Provide training on the software program used for observations.
- Arrange for release time when teachers are walking.
- Participate in observations.
- Prepare and oversee the sharing of observation data.
- Arrange for time and location for follow-up and sharing and debriefing of observation data.
- Develop the agenda for the classroom walkthrough team meeting.
- Assist with the development and monitoring of follow-up actions after the walkthroughs are complete.
- Acquire funding to support the process.
- Listen to and address staff concerns about the walks.
- Assist with the evaluation of the walkthrough process.

Tracking Walkthroughs

Tracking classroom visits is vital to ensure consistency, equity, quality, and fidelity of a walkthrough protocol. Who walks; who is visited; when walks occur; and what data are collected, organized, and reported or shared are all features of the tracking effort. Some schools we studied simply track observation data from previous walkthroughs as input to decisions on future school improvement and professional development efforts.

Other schools keep binders, notebooks, or logbooks for walkthrough tracking and record keeping. The principal at Ganado Intermediate School keeps a folder for each teacher that includes the checklist form, the walkthrough schedules, and lists of which classrooms are visited and which teachers participate.

At Oxford Academy, a lesson design notebook stores copies of the stated focus and targeted questions used for gathering data and a summary report of the data gathered from the walks. The school's lesson design specialist keeps this information in a working notebook as a data reference to determine the school's next steps in school improvement and to document information about its walkthrough practice.

Teachers at Huntingtown High School use a logbook to record walkthrough data. Teachers sign in to the logbook to verify that they have completed the required walkthrough. The log includes the names of observing teachers, host teachers, and the date and time of the walk.

Several schools track their walkthroughs by entering information into folders or spreadsheets on their computers. At Monitor Elementary School, the walkthrough days and times are posted on a master professional development calendar, documented in observation notes (observation teams, dates and times of the walks, and who was visited), and recorded on a master spreadsheet. At South Junior High School in Idaho, a teacher leader coordinates the walkthrough scheduling by recording who participated, when, and where. This ensures that all classrooms are visited for the same amount of time and that all participants have an opportunity to walk.

Schools using the Teachscape Walkthrough software, the McREL Power Walkthrough software, or the Look 2 Learning software have electronic templates available to them that track, record, store, and analyze observation data. The resulting reports contain data regarding who observes, how many times observers have been in a teacher's room, the date and time of the walkthrough, patterns observed, and subsequent changes in instruction and learning. Several schools use iPad applications that enable them to organize, identify, and clarify information and allow them to provide immediate feedback to teachers regarding observed instructional practices.

> I keep track of the teacher walkthroughs in a folder on my computer. I enter the schedule of visits, including room numbers, observers, times of visits, the "problem of practice," and the focus of the observations.
>
> —*Lorilyn Caron, Principal,*
> *Mohegan Elementary School*

Other strategies to track the walkthrough process and observation data in the schools we studied include the following:

- **Alan Shawn Feinstein Middle School**—The principal divides the school into sections and assigns pairs or groups of observers to each section for walkthrough observations. Walkthrough reports presented to the faculty include observation data, date of the walks, and observing participants.
- **Arroyo Vista Charter School**—The principal keeps a calendar to record the grade-level teams doing the visits and notes from each of the walkthroughs.
- **Belleville East and West High Schools**—A written record includes information about the type of class that is visited (department, core or elective, time of day).
- **Bridges High School**—The teaching staff reports on progress toward their four school goals. This self-report includes reflections on walkthroughs in which they participated.
- **Fort Vancouver High School**—A monthly instructional newsletter includes observation data that are compiled and reported by observing teachers.
- **James Hubert Blake High School**—Participants in walkthroughs turn in a reflection sheet to their resource teacher following a departmental debriefing session.
- **Martin Luther King, Jr. Middle School**—A printed schedule is distributed, which identifies the teams that will walk, classrooms team members who will observe, and who will lead the "hall talk" and team debriefs.
- **Parkway Elementary School**—The classroom walkthrough coordinators use charts to track teachers who walk, where they walk, when they walk, and the rooms visited.
- **South Junior High School, California**—The principal e-mails information about the schedule and focus question. After the observations, the principal again sends e-mails describing patterns noted in the observation data, sharing any questions that arise, and outlining next steps.

Announcing Walkthroughs

Another issue sometimes raised is whether walkthroughs should be announced in advance or conducted as unannounced events. We think the answer to this question resides in the responses to two other questions: (1) What is the purpose and expected outcome of your walks? and (2) What is the level of comfort and trust within your school setting? The majority of teachers at Jonesboro High School requested that walkthroughs be announced in advance. They felt that advance announcements would enable host teachers to plan lessons intentionally and carefully that exhibit the best instructional practices for others to witness. On the other hand, if your purpose is to acquire snapshots of all that occurs during the teaching day, then unannounced walkthroughs may provide more authentic data.

> When considering announcing teacher walkthroughs in advance, I believe that if you happen to see that teachers [present] "dog and pony" lessons during a rounds visit, it shows you what those teachers are truly capable of doing in the classroom.
>
> —*Brooke Puricelli, Principal,*
> *DeWitt Perry Middle School*

When considering the level of comfort and trust within your school setting, giving teachers advance notice that peers will be observing them may ease some anxiety. According to the principal at Belleville East High School, the purpose for initially announcing walkthroughs was to establish a comfort level among teachers until frequent classroom observations became part of the culture.

We found that most of the featured schools provide some kind of advance announcement that walkthroughs will be occurring. In some cases, the schedule of walkthroughs is prepared before the new school year. At Ball Junior High School, the walkthroughs are placed on the school's master at the beginning of the year, and all of the dates are shared in September. The same is true at South Junior High School in California, where a professional development calendar is created at the beginning of the year and includes the schedule of classroom walkthroughs. Before each walk, the date and focus question are communicated at staff meetings and through e-mails.

At Crystal River Elementary School, the school leadership team plans the walkthroughs and communicates related information through weekly staff memos. This communication informs all teachers about who will be observed, who will observe, and when staff outside the building will participate. For Summit Middle School, teachers volunteering to observe others are responsible for contacting the teachers to be observed to ask for permission and to share observation dates, purpose, and look-fors.

Connecting Walkthroughs to Other School Improvement Efforts

It is important that walkthroughs do not operate as a stand-alone school improvement effort. Schools need multiple ways to collect data on instruction and learning, and walkthroughs provide only one important data source. We asked featured schools, "How are walkthrough data connected with your other school data?" We learned that this connection was demonstrated in a variety of ways. The data collected by teachers observing one another were

- Correlated to students' formative and summative assessment data.
- Correlated to standardized test data.
- Compared with data collected from administrator walkthroughs.
- Related to data on attendance, demographics, and library usage.
- Aligned with reviews of course planning and the design of instructional materials.
- Connected with survey data from teachers on professional practice.
- Related to student and parental surveys about the school.
- Compared to action research on other school curricular and instructional initiatives.

We were also interested in how walkthroughs were integrated or aligned with other school improvement initiatives. We found the majority of schools connected their walkthroughs to one or more of the following: state-mandated initiatives, district and school improvement plans, professional development plans, and professional learning communities.

State-Mandated Initiatives

One example of the connection between walkthroughs and state-mandated initiatives is in the area of new teacher evaluation systems. Like many states, Arkansas is in the process of transitioning to a new teacher evaluation system. Although walkthroughs are not being used for teacher evaluation at Monitor Elementary School or Jonesboro High School, teachers at both schools are using the proposed teacher evaluation criteria as part of their focus and look-fors for walkthroughs. Walkthroughs provided an opportunity for teachers to become familiar with the evaluation criteria before they were fully implemented in the revised teacher evaluation process. Walkthroughs help teachers internalize best practices upon which they will be evaluated.

Tennessee has also designed a new teacher evaluation system. Griffith Elementary School had implemented the Instructional Rounds model (Marzano, Frontier, & Livingston, 2011) and, like the schools in Arkansas, used walkthroughs to prepare teachers for formal evaluation. The emphasis was on helping teachers become familiar with the teacher evaluation criteria by directly observing classroom practices during walkthroughs across the school.

District and School Improvement Plans

District and school improvement plans drive instructional and curricular initiatives to improve teaching and learning. We found many connections between such initiatives and walkthroughs. The staff at Salt Creek Elementary School is working to improve writing instruction as its schoolwide instructional goal, so the teacher walkthroughs focus on writing instruction. Professional conversations about classroom observations enable teachers to access ideas, strategies, and resources from one another to advance the writing initiative.

The walkthroughs at Alan Shawn Feinstein Middle School are designed to assess school improvement plans in the area of literacy teaching. They are a means to measure where the school is in terms of the instruction and assessment of literacy across the content areas.

Members of the school improvement team at Parkway Elementary School collect data on their school improvement goals to align with classroom walkthrough observations. Data aligned with their walkthroughs include evidence of children being respectful, applying higher-order thinking skills, and reflecting on their learning. The data are used to measure the school's focus as related to a school improvement goal written for that school year. Anecdotal data and performance-based information related to the school's focus serve as measures of impact.

Professional Development Plans

Plans for schoolwide professional development often inform the walkthrough focus. For example, walkthroughs at South Junior High School in Idaho help teachers decide upon the direction of their future professional development. This enables the principal to coordinate staff development by arranging and monitoring the training, setting up book studies, and leading other collaborative learning efforts.

The teaching staff at James Hubert Blake High School focus on studying and observing equitable teaching practices. They demand that teachers hold high expectations for every student. The walkthroughs address the extent to which instructional practice is equitable for all students. Walkthrough data provide direction for subsequent professional development aimed at helping teachers better understand what high expectations are and how they are conveyed to students.

Professional Learning Communities

A number of schools use walkthroughs to build professional learning communities. The purpose of Collaborative Learning Visits at Summit Middle School is to further the learning community initiative and promote schoolwide professional dialogue on curriculum, instruction, and assessment. The purpose is similar at Burlington High School, where staff members model a community of learners in their walkthrough process. They demonstrate that they value the process of learning by sharing their experiences with one another and engaging in meaningful discussions about what high-quality learning looks like.

The Montville School District in Connecticut brought in the UCLA Center X Classroom Walk-Through model to support the creation of professional learning communities in all of the schools. The walkthrough process implemented at two of the district's schools, Mohegan Elementary School and Leonard J. Tyl Middle School, serves as a means to improve instruction. Through the process, teachers become familiar with research-based instructional strategies and experience a collaborative teaching environment in which best practices are shared.

Evaluating the Walkthrough Process

Like any other school improvement initiative, it is critical that the walkthrough initiative include a built-in evaluation process to determine if it is meeting its purpose and expected outcomes. An evaluation will provide answers to questions about the efficacy of your walks. In our study, we asked schools about the evaluation of their walkthroughs (see the rubric in Figure 5.2), using a range with "No Evaluation" at one end and "Formal Evaluation" at the other. Most schools were concentrated at the "Informal Evaluation" stage, and the fewest were at the "Formal Evaluation" stage.

FIGURE 5.2
Rubric of Responses on School Evaluation of Walkthrough Process

0 No Evaluation	1 Anticipate Evaluation	2 Informal Evaluation	3 Formal Evaluation
No formal or informal evaluations in place for schools just starting the walkthroughs.	Some type of evaluation of the walkthroughs anticipated but not yet undertaken in schools implementing the process for several years.	Informal evaluations of walkthroughs occurring primarily through discussions in school leadership team meetings, staff meetings, departmental or grade-level meetings, or post-walkthrough debriefings and reflective conversations.	Evaluation questions about the walkthroughs being embedded in teacher surveys administered either semiannually or annually or through focus groups.

We highly recommend that every school that implements walkthroughs regularly evaluate the purpose, process, and expected outcomes. The evaluation should assess the degree to which the walkthrough protocol has been implemented as planned; attitudes of teachers and administrators toward the walkthroughs; ways to increase the value of the walkthroughs; and the impact of the walkthroughs on instruction and learning.

> The evaluations of our teacher walkthroughs have been rather informal and are often included as a part of the reflective conversations we hold following the walks. Changes in the way that our walkthroughs are conducted have and do occur as a result of this feedback.
>
> —*Maribel Childress, Principal, Monitor Elementary School*

We also recommend conducting a summative evaluation at least annually. Appendix I presents a proposed sample survey that can serve as a guide in designing an evaluation instrument. You can revise this survey so that it meets your purpose and your walkthrough protocols. Even the Likert scale ranging from "totally agree" to "totally disagree" can be changed to measure your school's requested feedback more accurately. A statement at the bottom of the survey asks for comments so teachers have an opportunity to share opinions or ask questions. Your school may choose to administer this survey electronically and ask for anonymous responses. Focus groups are another way to evaluate the impact of walkthroughs. You may use the items in the sample survey to facilitate the conversation.

Measuring Impact on Teaching and Learning

The purpose of professional development is to improve instruction and student learning. We asked the schools we studied how they determined the impact of walkthroughs on teaching and learning. Most said they measured this impact by observing changes in teaching practices and student learning during subsequent walkthroughs. As stated by a former principal at Ganado Intermediate School, "We look for the consistency of best instructional practices over time that serve as our focus and look-fors in our walkthroughs. If we see an increase in their application, our teaching staff knows we are having an impact on teaching and learning."

Monitor Elementary School uses its walkthroughs to collect data on the implementation of new professional development initiatives. The walkthrough observation data demonstrate how frequently teachers are using a particular strategy or instructional model for which they were professionally prepared. The school then correlates those findings with student assessment data to determine if improvements in student achievement have occurred.

Software programs for walkthrough observations provide summary reports on the effect on teaching and learning. The Teachscape observation software used at Jonesboro High School records evidence of instructional practices and delivers reports of observed patterns to show how teaching and learning are affected. The summary of walkthrough observation data enables Jonesboro teachers to implement, support, and sustain an effective lesson-planning model to improve teaching practice and student learning. The schools in Roaring Fork School District and Carman-Ainsworth School District use McREL's Power Walkthrough. This walkthrough observation software also delivers observation reports to the schools to help instructional leaders monitor changes over time in the context of instruction (for example, whole group, small groups, individual), the type of work students are producing, whether students are able to identify learning goals, and the kind of technology being used.

Several schools use perceptual or reflective surveys to measure the impact of walkthroughs on teaching and learning. Annual surveys at Fort Vancouver High School ask students and staff about learning. Students are asked to respond to statements such as "My teachers let me know what I'm expected to learn in class" and "It's easier for me to learn when I get a chance to reflect on my learning." Teachers provide feedback about the frequency of instructional strategies by responding to statements such as "I communicate learning targets to students on a daily basis" and "I use formative assessments that are aligned to my learning targets." The learning-walk data then allow staff to look for alignment between what actually happens in the classroom, what students and teachers say about what happens in the classroom, and what students and teachers say they want to see happen in the classroom. The school leadership team identifies gaps to use as opportunities for professional development as part of the school's improvement plan.

Teachers at South Junior High School in Idaho write their reflections on the Look 2 Learning walkthrough process and its effect on their teaching and student learning. The principal compiles the end-of-the-year comments into a written document and shares the summary report with staff at the beginning of the following school year. The reflections help guide any necessary changes to the walkthrough process.

Alan Shawn Feinstein Middle School uses a Literacy Walk Observation Survey to assess both classroom instruction and student learning. The questions focus primarily on formative assessment. As school principal Michael Almeida indicated,

> We know from research a teacher must use formative assessment practices to support student learning. Because our Literacy Walk reports are a collective assessment of our teaching and learning, our ability to measure the impact is limited to a schoolwide assessment. As part of the process, we include professional development. Together, they have had a tremendous impact on teaching and learning.

In summary, a number of the schools implementing teacher walkthroughs used a variety of formal and informal means to measure the impact on teaching and learning. Such measurement is best summarized by Jennifer Ortiz, a member of the professional development team at South Junior High School in California. She stated,

> For individual teachers who walk through the classrooms, there is certainly an impact on teaching, as this affords them a systematic view on the students' learning that they don't get during day-to-day instruction. The walkthrough is time to really think about students'

perceptions of what is being presented to them in the classroom. Those "a-ha" moments when participating in a walkthrough most definitely impact our teachers.

Lessons Learned and Moving Forward

As you decide which walkthrough process your school will implement and begin to plan how you will implement it, you need to address a number of additional issues to ensure success. Any new change effort in your school may be met with some degree of resistance. Introducing the concept of teacher participation in walkthroughs represents a major change in most schools. If your school has an established culture of trust in which teachers are motivated and included, then this resistance can be mitigated. It is critical to have regular, transparent communication and a system for teacher participation in the design, implementation, and evaluation of the walkthroughs. Careful attention to these processes will help teachers realize the value of observing and helping one another grow professionally through walkthroughs.

Teacher union issues also need to be considered. Teacher union concerns are reduced when teachers are actively involved in the design and implementation of walkthroughs, when teachers do not evaluate one another, and when participation in the process is strictly voluntary.

Successful implementation of a walkthrough initiative entails a multitude of ongoing coordination responsibilities. The principal may assume the lead or may find it more efficient and productive to delegate coordination to the school leadership team, a special walkthrough committee of teachers, or a few specific teachers.

Another issue for consideration is how walkthroughs complement performance data and improvement efforts. Schools collect data on teaching and learning in multiple ways, and walkthroughs provide additional data that corroborate with other student data.

Two evaluation issues to consider in the planning and implementation of your walkthroughs are (1) evaluating the process to determine if it is meeting the expected outcomes and (2) measuring the impact of the walkthroughs on teaching and learning. To measure whether the expected outcomes are being realized, the evaluation of the walkthrough process needs to be built in from the beginning and needs to be an ongoing process. Many schools use the informal evaluation process of discussing walkthroughs and their value during debriefs and reflective discussions by the observing team. Other schools use a survey or narrative form. The sample evaluation survey in Appendix I can help guide you in developing an instrument that reflects your school improvement goals.

Questions to Think About

- What are some strategies you might consider in convincing resistant or reluctant teaching colleagues to participate?
- Is your teacher union likely to have concerns about walkthroughs?
- Who will coordinate and track all of the aspects of the walkthroughs (such as the visitation schedule, communications, training, release time, participation, sharing of data, and evaluation)?
- How will walkthroughs contribute to other school data and complement other school improvement initiatives related to teaching and learning?
- How and when should you evaluate your walkthroughs?
- What are some areas of teaching and learning you hope will be affected by walkthroughs?

Our Recommendations

- Invite resistant or reluctant teachers to participate in walkthroughs at other schools to learn more about the experience and its value.
- Provide multiple opportunities for discussions about the value and implementation of the walkthrough process, ensuring that all teachers have an opportunity to participate.
- Involve teacher union leadership in the earliest exploration and planning of teacher walkthrough protocols.
- Align and connect the walkthroughs to areas of professional development the staff have participated in and to other school improvement initiatives.

- Consider an easy but informative electronic management system that allows you to track and keep a comprehensive record of walkthroughs.
- Continually monitor the walkthroughs to ensure that they are credible and valuable to all staff.
- Develop both formative and summative evaluations of your walkthroughs to assess and evaluate how well the process is meeting the intended purpose and outcomes.
- Determine how you will measure the impact on instruction and learning as a result of walkthroughs and the subsequent reflective discussions.
- Communicate the results of the walkthroughs relative to goals for classroom instruction and student achievement.
- Use walkthrough data to help determine the next steps for improving student achievement.

CHAPTER 6

Concluding Thoughts

I wonder how many children's lives might be saved if we educators disclosed what we know to each other.

—Roland Barth

There is no single, perfect plan for initiating walkthroughs because of variables such as school culture, goals, history, needs, and challenges at each school. The idea of teachers observing teachers may be a significant change in many schools. Each school must address how to start, whom to involve, what to consider in planning, what to focus on, and how to sustain the process. In this book, we have attempted to draw upon a broad range of schools that demonstrate varying levels of experience with walkthroughs. Each case had its own context and challenges, but the message of success is remarkably consistent. Every situation represented a school on a journey to change its culture by valuing teachers as professional partners in the classroom walkthrough endeavor. These schools recognized that improving teaching and learning does not occur by mandates, policies, edicts, or other outside demands. Working collaboratively, engaging in collegial inquiry, and searching and sharing evidence of effective teaching and learning practices through walkthroughs became part of their culture. Educators at these schools recognize that those closest to students always have the greatest impact on student learning.

Teachers react differently to the idea of becoming involved in walkthroughs. Some immediately find satisfaction in having expanded opportunities to learn from colleagues, whereas others are reluctant to open their classrooms to peer observers. The best way to ensure the success of any effort to introduce walkthroughs is to learn how your teachers think the process should be designed, what training they feel they need for conducting walkthroughs, and what they believe the walkthroughs should look like in practice and follow-up. We cannot overemphasize how crucial teacher input is to the planning and implementing of walkthrough protocols. Acceptance and investment in the process will occur only when colleagues value walkthroughs as a vehicle for improving their own teaching practices.

We want to share two other concluding thoughts with you. First, schools should revise their walkthrough protocols over time to ensure the process continues to meet their needs. Second, the introduction of the Common Core State Standards (CCSS) in many states has implications for walkthroughs.

We encountered a number of schools that regularly revise their walkthrough protocols to ensure that their original relevance, purpose, and outcomes continue to meet expectations. Schools make changes in the observation forms they use, in how the reflective conversations are held, and occasionally in the name of the walkthrough process to describe its purpose more accurately.

As staff at Crownhill Elementary School reviewed their walkthrough protocol, they decided to eliminate the checklist they had used for taking observation notes and replace it with just taking objective notes of what was observed. At Katella High School, the staff narrowed the observation form so it was more focused on what to observe. They considered their original form to be too general to provide helpful data. The staff at Salt Creek Elementary School participated in training to learn reflective coaching and questioning. They used their new skills in walkthrough debriefs.

The first three years of Monitor Elementary School's walkthroughs were conducted in horizontal walking teams of teachers, so the reflective conversations were always with grade-level peers. From the informal evaluation of the walks, teachers realized that this configuration never allowed them to observe grade-level peers. The teachers asked for opportunities to conduct walks in both vertical and horizontal teams so they could get a broader view of instruction throughout the school.

Beginning in the 2012–2013 school year, schools in Anaheim Union High School District made major changes in the teacher walkthrough protocols. They now refer to their walkthroughs as "learning walks," and all of the schools in the district follow the same protocol. The district created a new template to guide observations and conversations after the walks. The focus of the walks includes all of the elements of an effective lesson as determined by the district, including the Common Core State Standards. The form contributes to reflective discussions that are more content focused among teachers conducting walks. Those teachers walk in groups of four to six over an entire day with a trained facilitator, visiting classrooms for 10 to 15 minutes each. Teachers record their observations after leaving the classroom, writing "I observed . . ." and "I heard . . ." statements. Immediately following each classroom visit, the group engages in a reflective discussion about what they observed before moving on to the next classroom. Each discussion ends with every teacher making an "I" statement about what he or she will commit to replicating in the classroom based on his or her observations. For those schools, the walkthroughs become real-time professional development for the walkers.

These examples illustrate that when the intent and value of the walkthroughs are not being fully met in light of school improvement goals and needs, it is very important to make adjustments to the protocols.

Our final thought is about the relationship between the Common Core State Standards and walkthroughs. As of the 2011–2012 school year, none of our featured schools included the standards as a focus for their teacher walkthroughs, but many of them indicated that they intend to include CCSS as an area of focus in the near future. Therefore, we mention the standards as a broad area of focus for walkthroughs in the coming years.

The CCSS represent a major paradigm shift in the design of K–12 curriculum and instructional delivery. These national education standards represent a set of shared goals and expectations for what students should understand and be able to do in grades K–12 in order to be prepared for success in college and the workplace. Compared to current standards in most states, the CCSS are based on very different theories and approaches to teaching. At present, teachers are not fully prepared, and most textbooks and related resources in use today are inconsistent or inadequate when it comes to supporting and implementing the CCSS. Teachers will need substantial professional development on the standards, instruction, resources, and assessments to support the scope of changes called for with these standards.

To adequately implement the CCSS, a plan of action beyond just raising awareness will need to include long-range, comprehensive professional learning opportunities and collaboration to prepare staff for changes in the curriculum, instruction, and assessments schoolwide. ASCD conducted a Common Core State Standards Survey at their 2012 annual conference and surveyed a sample of ASCD members to learn more about what schools were doing or planning to do about CCSS implementation. Sixty-eight percent of the respondents replied that ongoing, job-embedded professional development was the only way to ensure alignment of instructional practices.

A number of different types of collaborative, job-embedded professional learning activities for the CCSS can improve teacher practice and student achievement. We suggest that one of the most powerful learning activities is walkthroughs. Classroom walkthroughs launch and support opportunities for teachers to work together as a community during the school day. Through the walkthrough experience, teachers make connections by observing one another's CCSS practices (see examples of teacher walkthrough observation forms that address the CCSS in Appendix G), conducting professional conversations with one another, and furthering the development of their own knowledge and skills in CCSS teaching practices. Because the common core will be new to everyone, observing, discussing, and establishing new practices will be crucial to student success. An ideal process for implementing this change is classroom walkthroughs.

Classroom walkthroughs represent embedded professional development and growth of the highest quality because they are

- Focused on individual and schoolwide improvement.
- Respectful of the intellectual expertise and leadership capacity of teachers.
- Collaborative in nature, with teachers helping one another with professional growth opportunities.
- Ongoing, intensive, and integral to the regular workday of teachers.
- Immediately connected with authentic student learning.
- Relevant and of instant value for direct application of ideas to classroom practices.
- Cost-effective and efficient in terms of the impact on teaching and learning.
- Evaluated directly on the basis of impact on teacher effectiveness and student learning.

As your school moves its students toward the same educational goals, it makes sense for your teaching colleagues to share CCSS ideas, instructional strategies, and reflections with one another through classroom walkthroughs and subsequent discussions. The meaningful sharing of ideas and experiences through walkthroughs will be crucial to building a collective understanding of what the common core looks like in the classroom. The ultimate outcome is to assist all teaching colleagues in the uncharted waters of the CCSS.

In closing, we reiterate that classroom walkthroughs are a powerful tool to add to your school's professional development repertoire. When teachers are an integral part of the process, walkthroughs are even more effective in supporting student achievement. Reflective dialogues following walkthroughs provide opportunities for professional colleagues to encourage and support learning and growth among their peers. We want educators to gain ideas from the schools featured in this book. Their experiences will make your planning, implementing, and institutionalizing of classroom walkthroughs much easier.

We hope this book has piqued your interest and motivation to learn more about the walkthrough process. Our vision is that every school will become a learning community in which all of its educators continually engage in inquiry, sharing, problem solving, and reflection for the benefit of all students.

APPENDIX A

Featured Schools and Demographics

School	Grades	Number of Students	Number of Staff	Racial/Ethnic Mix	Free/ Reduced Lunch Population
Alan Shawn Feinstein Middle School Coventry Public Schools of Rhode Island Coventry, Rhode Island (401) 822-9426	6–8	1,188	84	95% Caucasian 5% Other	29%
Arroyo Vista Charter School Chula Vista Elementary School District Chula Vista, California (619) 656-9676	K–6	828	36	48% Hispanic 26% Caucasian 21% Asian/Pacific Islander 4% African-American 1% Other	15%
Ball Junior High School Anaheim Union High School District Anaheim, California (714) 999-3663	7–8	1,218	53	50% Hispanic 37% Caucasian 11% Asian/Pacific Islander 2% African-American	81%
Basalt Middle School Roaring Fork School District Carbondale, Colorado (970) 384-5900	5–8	406	27	57% Hispanic 40% Caucasian 3% Other	50%
Belleville East High School Belleville Township High School District 201 Belleville, Illinois (618) 222-3700	9–12	2,688	149	52% Caucasian 37% African American 11% Other	35%

continued

School	Grades	Number of Students	Number of Staff	Racial/Ethnic Mix	Free/Reduced Lunch Population
Belleville West High School Belleville Township High School District 201 Belleville, Illinois (618) 222-7500	9–12	2,277	119	62% Caucasian 31% African American 7% Other	40%
Benton Grade School K–4 Benton School District 47 Benton, Illinois (618) 438-7181	PK–4	687	38	96% Caucasian 4% Other	64%
Bridges High School Roaring Fork School District Carbondale, Colorado (970) 384-6160	9–12	80	6	48% Caucasian 44% Hispanic 8% Other	30%
Burlington High School Burlington Public Schools Burlington, Massachusetts (781) 270-1836	9–12	1,111	85	78% Caucasian 12% Asian/Pacific Islander 6% African American 4% Other	10%
Cheney Middle School Cheney Public Schools Cheney, Washington (509) 559-4409	6–8	882	49	76% Caucasian 9% Hispanic 3% Asian/Pacific Islander 12% Other	45%
Cleveland High School Seattle Public Schools Seattle, Washington (206) 252-7800	9–12	738	39	44% African American 37% Asian/Pacific 12% Hispanic 7% Other	70%
Crownhill Elementary School Bremerton School District Bremerton, Washington (360) 473-4200	K–5	419	26	60% Caucasian 16% Hispanic 3% African-American 21% Other	58%
Crystal River Elementary School Roaring Fork School District Carbondale, Colorado (970) 384-5620	PK–4	450	37	72% Hispanic 25% Caucasian 3% Other	62%

School	Grades	Number of Students	Number of Staff	Racial/Ethnic Mix	Free/ Reduced Lunch Population
DeWitt Perry Middle School Carrollton–Farmers Branch Independent School District Carrollton, Texas (972) 968-4400	6–8	933	66	80% Hispanic 10% Caucasian 10% Other	85%
Dr. Charles E. Murphy Elementary School Montville Public Schools Oakdale, Connecticut (860) 848-9241	PK–5	383	29	75% Caucasian 9% Hispanic 3% Asian/Pacific Islander 13% Other	33%
Edmonton Public Schools* Edmonton, Alberta Canada (780) 438-5011	NA	NA	NA	NA	NA
E. R. Geddes Elementary School Baldwin Park Unified School District Baldwin, California (626) 962-8114	K–5	703	37	91% Hispanic 6% Asian/Pacific Islander 3% Other	87%
Fontana Unified School District** Fontana, California (909) 357-5000	NA	NA	NA	NA	NA
Fort Vancouver High School Vancouver Public Schools Vancouver, Washington (360) 313-4000	9–12	1,398	63	57% Caucasian 26% Hispanic 8% Asian/Pacific 6% African-American 3% Other	67%
Ganado Intermediate School Ganado Unified School District 20 Ganado, Arizona (928) 755-1310	4–6	322	18	96% Native American 4% Other	99%
Griffith Elementary School Sequatchie County Schools Dunlap, Tennessee (423) 949-2105	PK–4	936	62	89% Caucasian 6% Latino/Hispanic 5% Other	72%

continued

School	Grades	Number of Students	Number of Staff	Racial/Ethnic Mix	Free/ Reduced Lunch Population
Huntingtown High School Calvert County Public Schools Huntingtown, Maryland (410) 414-7036	9–12	1,676	93	81% Caucasian 12% African American 7% other	10%
James Hubert Blake High School Montgomery County Public Schools Silver Spring, Maryland (301) 879-1300	9–12	1,872	103	43% African American 27% Caucasian 19% Hispanic 9% Asian/Pacific Islander 2% Other	27%
Jonesboro High School Jonesboro School District Jonesboro, Arkansas (870) 933-5881	10–12	1,066	76	52% Caucasian 41% African American 6% Hispanic 1% Other	58%
Katella High School Anaheim Union High School District Anaheim, California (714) 999-3621	9–12	2,690	93	84% Hispanic 9% Caucasian 5% Asian/Pacific Islander 2% Other	72%
Lancaster High School Antelope Valley Union High School District Lancaster, California (661) 726-7649	8–12	2,459	106	43% Hispanic 26% Caucasian 24% African American 5% Asian/Pacific Islander 2% Other	55%
Leonard J. Tyl Middle School Montville Public Schools Oakdale, Connecticut (860) 848-2822	6–8	642	53	73% Caucasian 8% Asian/Pacific Islander 8% Hispanic 11% Other	27%
Martin Luther King, Jr. Middle School Prince George's County Public Schools Beltsville, Maryland (301) 572-0650	6–8	689	54	58% African American 17% Hispanic 11% Caucasian 9% Asian/Pacific Islander 5% Other	44%

School	Grades	Number of Students	Number of Staff	Racial/Ethnic Mix	Free/ Reduced Lunch Population
Mohegan Elementary School Montville Public Schools Oakdale, Connecticut (860) 848-9261	PK–5	419	30	53% Caucasian 19% Asian/Pacific Islander 8% Hispanic 5% African American 15% Other	34%
Monitor Elementary School Springdale Public Schools Springdale, Arkansas (479) 750-8749	PK–5	808	42	42% Hispanic 38% Caucasian 15% Asian/Pacific Islander 5% Other	80%
Munford Elementary School Talladega County Schools Talladega, Alabama (256) 315-5250	K–5	710	54	76% Caucasian 21% African American 3% Hispanic	74%
Oxford Academy Anaheim Union High School District Anaheim, California (714) 220-3055	7–12	1,128	43	70% Asian/Pacific Islander 14% Hispanic 12% Caucasian 4% Other	28%
Parkway Elementary School Greenwich Public Schools Greenwich, Connecticut (203) 869-7466	K–5	292	26	82% Caucasian 10% Hispanic 4% Asian/Pacific Islander 4% Other	4%
Randels Elementary School Carman-Ainsworth Community Schools Flint, Michigan (810) 591-3250	K–5	528	31	53% African American 33% Caucasian 5% Hispanic 9% Other	65%
Salt Creek Elementary School Chula Vista Elementary School District Chula Vista, California (619) 397-5494	K–6	975	44	49% Hispanic 20% Caucasian 19% Asian/Pacific Islander 12% Other	9%

continued

School	Grades	Number of Students	Number of Staff	Racial/Ethnic Mix	Free/ Reduced Lunch Population
Schubert Elementary School Chicago Public Schools Chicago, Illinois (773) 534-3080	PK–5	989	45	92% Hispanic 3% Caucasian 2% African American 3% Other	99%
South Junior High School Anaheim Union High School District Anaheim, California (714) 999-3667	6–9	1,502	68	85% Hispanic 10% Caucasian 4% Asian/Pacific Islander 1% Other	85%
South Junior High School Boise School District Boise, Idaho (208) 854-6110	7–9	636	42	74% Caucasian 15% Hispanic 6% African American 4% Asian/Pacific Islander 1% Other	72%
Summit Middle School Southwest Allen County Schools Fort Wayne, Indiana (260) 431-2502	6–8	720	40	87% Caucasian 5% Hispanic 3% African American 5% Other	16%
Williamsport Area High School Williamsport Area School District Williamsport, Pennsylvania (570) 323-8411	9–12	1,715	124	72% Caucasian 22% African American 6% Other	50%

* Six elementary schools of the Edmonton Public Schools in Canada are involved with a teacher walk-through process known as "Instructional Talk-Throughs."

** All of the schools of Fontana Unified School District are involved with walkthroughs for new teachers. Teachers conduct intervisitations across the entire school district.

Appendix B

Study Questions for Schools with Teacher Walkthroughs

Initial Study Questions (Round One):

1. What are the **demographics** of your school (urban, suburban, or rural; grades; enrollment; number of certified staff; racial/ethnic mix; percent of free/reduced lunch)?

2. What **name** do you use for your walkthroughs (e.g., Learning Walks, Collaborative Walkthroughs, Instructional Walkthroughs, Focused Walks)?

3. What is/are the **purpose(s)** of your walkthrough model?

4. **How long** have walkthroughs been implemented in your school?

5. **Who actually participates** as observers (e.g., building team leaders, teacher leaders, coaches, instructional specialists, all teachers)?

6. How **often** are walks conducted, and what is the average **length of time** spent in a classroom?

7. What are the specific **focus(es) and look-fors** in your walkthrough model?

8. What were the **sources** used to determine the walkthrough focus and look-fors?

9. What kind of **observation form** (checklist, note taking, combination of both) or **software program/ technology** do you use to record/report data?

10. Are **observations recorded** as to just what was observed, or do they include evaluative statements (e.g., good review lesson, excellent classroom management, questions asked were very good)?

11. How is **observation feedback** given? Describe the steps or process.

12. What has been the **role and responsibility of the principal** in supporting/sustaining the walkthrough model involving teachers?

13. **Who coordinates** the whole walkthrough process for your school?

14. Do you have a way for walkthroughs to be **tracked** (who, when, where)? If yes, how do you keep track of the process?

15. Do you **evaluate your walkthrough model** as to whether it is meeting expectations on how it is conducted and valued? If yes, how and how often?

16. What **other data** do you gather and analyze to complement evidence collected from walkthroughs?

17. Do you try to determine or **measure the impact on teaching and learning** based on the walkthroughs conducted? If yes, how do you do this?

continued

Follow-up Study Questions (Round Two):

1. What was the **catalyst or reason(s) for walkthroughs** to be considered for implementation in your school?

2. **How did the process begin?** Where did it start, and who was important in championing the effort?

   a. What were some of the very important **initial steps** in getting walkthroughs implemented?

   b. How were **teachers first approached** on the idea of becoming involved in walkthroughs?

   c. How were **teachers' anxiety and reluctance** addressed?

3. What features of your **school's culture** needed to be in place for walkthroughs to be accepted and valued?

4. How was a **level of trust** achieved to ensure that walkthroughs would be successful?

5. What **issues or obstacles** arose when classroom teachers became involved as observers? More specifically, what have been the risks of having teachers observing colleagues?

6. Are there **"walking norms"** or **ground rules** created that guide the teachers' walking process and behavioral expectations?

7. How are teachers who conduct walkthroughs **selected**?

8. Describe what had to be done to **schedule times** for teachers to conduct walks and reflective conversations.

9. What **other issues** had to be addressed in allowing teachers opportunities to conduct walks and have professional conversations?

10. If applicable, what **preparation/training** was provided for teachers who conducted the walks?

11. How did teachers **prefer to receive feedback**?

12. Aside from teacher feedback, what **other follow-up efforts** are undertaken from the walkthrough observation data collected?

13. How are the walkthroughs **connected, related, or coordinated with other school improvement efforts/initiatives** (e.g., book studies, joint lesson planning, group analysis of student work, mentoring, coaching, embedded professional development)?

14. Has the **purpose for the walkthrough process in your school changed** from the first year of implementation? If yes, how has it changed and what contributed to the change?

15. Were there any **teacher union bargaining issues** you had to address? If so, what were they?

16. Are walkthroughs **announced in advance**?

17. From your perspective, what's been the **impact and/or benefit** of walkthroughs on

    a. Teachers

    b. Students

    c. School

    d. Others

18. What has been necessary to be able to **sustain the teacher walkthroughs** over time?

19. What **recommendations** would you give to schools and school districts considering teachers as observers in the walkthrough process?

Appendix C

Teacher Survey on Classroom Walkthroughs

The purpose of this survey is to acquire a profile of views about classroom walkthroughs that would be helpful in the design of our school's walkthrough model. Classroom walkthroughs are brief, frequent, informal, nonevaluative visits conducted throughout the school.

DIRECTIONS: Please respond to each of the questions below. For each question, you are given the opportunity to add any further comments.

1. What should be the **PURPOSE** of classroom walkthroughs? PLEASE NUMERICALLY RANK ALL OF THE OPTIONS, WITH 1 BEING THE HIGHEST-RANKED ITEM.

	Promote collegial conversations that become part of our school's professional learning culture.
	Increase schoolwide reflection on best practices to increase student achievement.
	Collect data to assist in decisions regarding continuous school improvement needs.
	Identify the professional development needs of the faculty and staff.
	Collect additional data on teaching practices and students' learning to supplement knowledge about how the school and students are performing.
	Appraise how professional development initiatives are being incorporated into classroom practices.
	Other (please specify):

Comments: _____

_____

_____

_____

_____

_____

continued

2. What should be the **FOCUS** of classroom walkthroughs in our school? PLEASE NUMERICALLY RANK ALL OF THE OPTIONS, WITH 1 BEING THE HIGHEST-RANKED ITEM.

	Teacher instructional practices
	Implementation of curricular initiatives
	Assessment techniques
	Student behavior
	Student learning activities
	Classroom environment (e.g., instructional resources, wall displays, etc.)
	Classroom management
	Other (please specify):

Comments: _____

_____

3. Should classroom walkthroughs be **ANNOUNCED** in advance?

_____ Yes   _____ No

Comments: _____

_____

4. How **FREQUENTLY** should classroom walkthroughs occur? CIRCLE ONLY ONE OPTION.

   a. Once annually

   b. Once a semester

   c. Once a quarter

   d. Once a month

   e. Twice a month

   f. Once a week

Comments: _____

_____

_____

_____

_____

_____

_____

5. How much **TIME** should observers spend in each classroom during the walks? CIRCLE ONLY ONE OPTION.

    a. 1–4 minutes

    b. 5–7 minutes

    c. 8–10 minutes

    d. 11–15 minutes

    e. More than 15 minutes

Comments: _____

_____

6. What should we **NAME** our classroom walkthroughs? CIRCLE ONLY ONE OPTION.

    a. Learning walks

    b. Professional learning visits

    c. Collaborative walks

    d. Instructional walks

    e. Other: (Please specify): _____

7. Should observers **TALK WITH STUDENTS** about what they are learning during classroom walkthroughs?

    _____ Yes   _____ No

Comments: _____

_____

8. How might observation data be **RECORDED** during classroom walkthroughs? CIRCLE ONLY ONE OPTION.

    a. Observers only use a checklist of what they observe.

    b. Observers only write notes about what they observe.

    c. Observers use a combination of checklist and note taking.

Comments: _____

_____

9. Should observers **RECORD** their walkthrough observations while in the classroom or after their departure? SELECT ONLY ONE OPTION.

_____ Inside classroom   _____ Outside classroom   _____ No preference

Comments: _____

_____

continued

10. Should it be **REQUIRED** that all of the school's staff participate in classroom walkthroughs?

_____ Yes   _____ No

Comments: _____

_____

11. How would you prefer that **OBSERVATION DATA** be shared? CIRCLE ALL THAT APPLY.

   a. Individual face-to-face

   b. Handwritten note or e-mail

   c. Department/grade level face-to-face sharing

   d. Whole-faculty face-to-face sharing

   e. Department written summary of observations

   f. Whole-school written summary of observations

   g. No sharing

Comments: _____

_____

12. What **NORMS OR GUIDELINES** should observers follow during the classroom walkthroughs (e.g., no cell phone conversations, no talking with students during direct instruction, etc.)?

_____

_____

_____

_____

13. What other **PERSPECTIVES** would you like to share about classroom walkthroughs?

_____

_____

_____

_____

14. What **NEEDS TO HAPPEN** for classroom walkthroughs to be an effective professional learning experience for all of our staff?

_____

_____

_____

_____

APPENDIX D

Walkthrough Models

Data-in-a-Day	http://www.aimcenterseattle.org/motivation/diad
Instructional Practices Inventory (IPI) Process	http://education.missouri.edu/orgs/mlic/4A_ipi_overview.php
Instructional Rounds Network	City, E. A., Elmore, R. F., Fiarman, S. E., & Teitel, L. (2009). *Instructional rounds in education: A network approach to improving teaching and learning.* Cambridge, MA: Harvard Education Press.
Instructional Rounds	Marzano, R. J., Frontier, T., & Livingston, D. (2011). *Effective supervision: Supporting the art and science of teaching.* Alexandria, VA: ASCD. Marzano, R. J. (2011, February). Making the most of instructional rounds. *Educational Leadership, 68*(5), 80–81.
Learning Walk Routine	http://ifl.lrdc.pitt.edu/ifl/index.php/professional_development/custom_training
Look 2 Learning (L2L)	http://colleaguesoncall.com/look2learning.html
McREL Power Walkthrough	http://www.mcrel.org/powerwalkthrough
Teachscape's *Reflect* Classroom Walkthrough	http://www.teachscape.com/products/reflect/how-it-works/walkthroughs
UCLA Center X Classroom Walk-Throughs	Martinez-Miller, P., & Cervone, L. (2008). *Breaking through to effective teaching: A walk-through protocol linking student practice and professional practice.* Lanham, MD: Rowman & Littlefield Education.

Sources of Focus/Look-fors and Observation Focus Areas

School	Sources of Focus/Look-fors	Observation Focus Areas
Alan Shawn Feinstein Middle School Coventry Public Schools (Rhode Island)	Rhode Island PreK–12 Literacy Policy Guidance; district and school improvement plans	Student engagement, questioning strategies, formative assessment, RTI, gradual release of responsibility
Arroyo Vista Charter School Chula Vista Elementary School District (California)	Everything viewed through the lens of English language learners and formative assessment data	Productive student work, guided instruction, gradual release of responsibility, written use of objectives, mathematics
Ball Junior High School Anaheim Union High School District (California)	Districtwide initiatives for school improvement	Student focused: "What evidence do we see/hear that students are . . ." (changing focus question for different walks)
Basalt Middle School Roaring Fork School District (Colorado)	*Classroom Instruction That Works* (Dean et al., 2012); Bloom's taxonomy; use of technology; context of learning	*CITW*'s strategies, levels of Bloom's taxonomy, uses of technology, grouping of students, articulation of learning goals
Belleville East High School Belleville Township High School District 201 (Illinois)	Instructional Practices Inventory Rubric on Student Engagement	Level of student engagement
Belleville West High School Belleville Township High School District 201 (Illinois)	Instructional Practices Inventory Rubric on Student Engagement	Level of student engagement
Benton Grade School K–4 Benton School District 47 (Illinois)	Gretchen Courtney strategies for reading comprehension	Reading comprehension strategies of predicting, summarizing, connecting, questioning, inferring, and imaging
Bridges High School Alternative High School Roaring Fork School District (Colorado)	Roaring Fork School District template on effective learning based on review by Colorado Department of Education	*CITW*'s strategies, levels of Bloom's taxonomy, uses of technology, grouping of students, articulation of learning goals

School	Sources of Focus/Look-fors	Observation Focus Areas
Burlington High School Burlington Public Schools (Massachusetts)	School improvement plan	Lesson objective clear to students, level of critical thinking, level of student engagement
Cheney Middle School Cheney Public Schools (Washington)	Responses from the Instructional Team Surveys	Positive behavior, aligned instruction, student engagement, student-centered assessment, assessment of learning
Cleveland High School Seattle Public Schools (Washington)	Four conditions for culturally responsive, motivating instruction	Rubrics for inclusion, positive attitude, conviction that learning has meaning, belief in students' competence
Crownhill Elementary School Bremerton School District (Washington)	STAR Learning Protocol; curriculum and instructional initiatives	Positive behavior, aligned instruction, student engagement, student-centered assessment, assessment of learning
Crystal River Elementary School Roaring Fork School District (Colorado)	School improvement plan; *Classroom Instruction That Works* (Dean et al., 2012)	Bloom's taxonomy, differentiation, scaffolding for language, time-on-task, student engagement, purposeful talk
DeWitt Perry Middle School Carrollton–Farmers Branch Independent School District (Texas)	State testing data, MAP data, observation data, data from previous rounds visits	Questions being asked; student explaining and defending their thinking; ratio of student talk to teacher talk
Dr. Charles E. Murphy Elementary School Montville Public Schools (Connecticut)	Previous walkthroughs, student test data, or school improvement initiative	Different focus question for each walkthrough
Edmonton Public Schools* (Canada)	Host teachers develop observation questions on which they want visiting teachers to focus	Student engagement, assessment, differentiation, use of technology
E. R. Geddes Elementary School Baldwin Park Unified School District (California)	School Leadership Team focus on student engagement/learning	Student focused: "What evidence do we see/hear that students are . . ." (changing focus question for different walks)
Fontana Unified School District** (California)	California Beginning Teacher Support and Assistance (BTSA) program standards	Focus areas aligned with the California Beginning Teacher Support and Assistance (BTSA) program standards
Fort Vancouver High School Vancouver Public Schools (Washington)	Locally reviewed research supporting constructivist teaching and Understanding by Design	Learning target posted and aligned to class activities, student engagement, and high levels of thinking
Ganado Intermediate School Native American School Ganado Unified School District 20 (Arizona)	Research on effective teaching	Locally designed 11-point checklist based on a review of research on effective teaching

School	Sources of Focus/Look-fors	Observation Focus Areas
Griffith Elementary School Sequatchie County Schools (Tennessee)	Marzano's observation protocol; statewide standards; district curriculum	Objectives, common core standards, activities in questioning, whatever the team of teachers desire to observe
Huntingtown High School Calvert County Public Schools (Maryland)	Feedback from the teaching staff surveys on their instructional needs	Classroom environment, student engagement, lesson closure, levels of questioning, types of teaching activities
James Hubert Blake High School Montgomery County Public Schools (Maryland)	Equitable classroom practices; student data; goals and objectives of school improvement plan	Student engagement with particular focus on personal relationships, classroom climate, and expectations
Jonesboro High School Jonesboro School District (Arkansas)	*Classroom Instruction That Works* (Dean et al., 2012)	Observations of instruction (*CITW* strategies and level of Bloom's taxonomy)
Katella High School Anaheim Union High School District (California)	Research from Doug Reeves, Robert Marzano, Rick DuFour, and the UCLA Center X Classroom Walk-Throughs	Learning and language objectives, checking for understanding, and oral academic discourse
Lancaster High School Antelope Valley Union High School District (California)	Site plan for student achievement; student work; benchmark results; and standardized test results	Departmental SMART goals, including indicators/steps/ instructional strategies and student engagement
Leonard J. Tyl Middle School Montville Public Schools (Connecticut)	Collaborative input and required readings during the UCLA Center X Classroom Walk-Through workshops and PLC initiatives	Student engagement, interdisciplinary connections, classroom management
Martin Luther King, Jr. Middle School Prince George's County Public Schools (Maryland)	Student data; Principles of Learning; research-based instructional practices; professional development needs	Instructional practices, differentiated grouping of students, assessing learner needs
Mohegan Elementary School Montville Public Schools (Connecticut)	*Classroom Instruction That Works* (Dean et al., 2012) & the National School Reform Faculty, Harmony Education Center	Problem of practice determined by the faculty prior to walkthroughs
Monitor Elementary School Springdale Public Schools (Arkansas)	Professional development initiatives; data from prior classroom walkthroughs; and student achievement data	Demonstration/evidence of best practices in instructional delivery and assessment

School	Sources of Focus/Look-fors	Observation Focus Areas
Munford Elementary School Talladega County Schools (Alabama)	Professional development	Formative assessment and student engagement
Oxford Academy Anaheim Union High School District (California)	School district initiatives	Students' accountable talk, using daily content objectives and language objectives
Parkway Elementary School Greenwich Public Schools (Connecticut)	Performance data collected for School Improvement Team Plan and on teacher interests	Social skills, higher-level thinking skills, synthesizing information, students reflecting on their learning
Randels Elementary School Carman-Ainsworth Community Schools (Michigan)	School improvement plan	Student engagement, school improvement strategies, student grouping patterns, instructional practices and assessment
Salt Creek Elementary School Chula Vista Elementary School District (California)	Current schoolwide instructional focus	Instructional strategies—e.g., Board Math, and shared and modeled writing
Schubert Elementary School Chicago Public Schools (Illinois)	Illinois State Board of Education Internal Review Process and TLC Model; Continuum of Literacy Learning	Targeted Instructional Area (TIA), guided reading
South Junior High School Anaheim Union High School District (California)	Annual school improvement objectives of the school; results from previous classroom walk-throughs	Student focused: "What evidence do we see/hear that students are . . ." (changing focus question for different walks)
South Junior High School Boise School District (Idaho)	Research of Bloom, M. Hunter, R. Stiggins, P. Schlechty, and R. Marzano	Objectives, thinking level, concept development and attainment, assessment, engagement, environment, and standards
Summit Middle School Southwest Allen County Schools (Indiana)	Goals/components of the School Improvement Plan	Learning environment, relationships, relevance, engagement, and student collaboration
Williamsport Area High School Williamsport Area School District (Pennsylvania)	Previous experience, Fullan System Reform Model, Principles of Learning (U. of Pittsburgh), *Classroom Instruction That Works* (Dean et al., 2012)	Authentic implementation of school's instructional design model with focus on a comprehensive literacy model

APPENDIX F

Examples of Walkthrough Observation Forms

Salt Creek Elementary School		
Board Math Feedback From		

Date: _____ Room Number: _____ Grade _____

Teacher: _____ Observer _____

Criteria	Observable Evidence	Wonderings
No. of problems 4–10 (5 days/week)		
All math strands are represented within two weeks. Number Sense; Algebra and Functions; Measurement and Geometry; Statistics, and Data Analysis and Probability		
Question stems taken from a variety of sources. CST Released Test Questions; District Math Benchmarks; Algebra Resource Binder; HM Practice and Challenge Problems		
Academic vocabulary is present. For example, *exponents*, *numerator*, *denominator*.		
Teacher models thinking process. "I" statements		

Criteria	Observable Evidence	Wonderings
Students engage with mental math. Use white boards judiciously; Choral response; TPR		
Previewed (33%) and reviewed rigorous problems		
Problem solving strategy used (2–5 problems a week)		
Rapid pacing (10–15 minutes) Use timer; Keep no. of problems manageable; Engage quickly		
Overall Comments:		

Source: Used with permission from Salt Creek Elementary School, Chula Vista, California.

Learning Visit Notes

Summit's superior instruction promotes learning and individual growth so that students are able to solve problems and change the world.

Most important things to promote student learning	What did it look like?
Learning Environment	
Relationships	
Relevance	
Engagement	
Student Collaboration	

Questions I have about the learning I see:

What I learned (or would like to learn more about) from my visit:

Source: Used with permission from Summit Middle School, Fort Wayne, Indiana.

Reflection Sheet for Walkthrough Observations Focusing on Student Learning

Evidence that students are accessing their prior knowledge.

Not today   Clearly Observable

- -

Evidence students are provided opportunities for both formal and informal formative assessment. Students' needs and interests based upon formative assessment are addressed.

Not today   Clearly Observable

- -

Evidence of students participating in developing assessment criteria.

Not today   Clearly Observable

- -

Evidence of students receiving and providing feedback to peers.

Not today   Clearly Observable

- -

Evidence of students working collaboratively to self-assess, set learning goals, and monitor their learning.

Not today   Clearly Observable

- -

Source: Used with permission from Cheney Middle School, Cheney, Washington.

APPENDIX G

Common Core Walkthrough Observation Forms

Classroom Walkthrough Observation Form	
Language and Literacy	

Observation Date: _____ Grade Level/Subject: 5th Grade Reading

Standards: Language and Literacy: Reading Standards for Literature K–5

Major Topic: Integration of Knowledge and Ideas

Anchor Standard: Compare and contrast stories in the same genre (e.g., mysteries and adventure stories) on their approaches to similar themes and topics.

Observation Notes	Ideas and Questions
Students read complex reading material from several varieties of text structure, such as narrative, cause and effect, and compare and contrast.	Not to use the text as a reference as opposed to it being used as a source of information.
Students were asked questions that drew upon their own experiences and background, but they were also asked to share evidence from the reading materials.	Base conversations on students' own experience and background, but balance that with information from the other resources.
Multiple sources (text, visuals, auditory) were used to integrate information on comparing mysteries.	What earlier strategies in reading were used to help students read complex materials?
Background knowledge of the students was used to illuminate the text but not replace it.	

Interactions with Students (Notes)

Students were able to explicitly state the standard related to today's lesson.

Students appeared to understand the connection between this lesson and the unit on nonfiction stories from the first quarter.

NOTE: This form would require the host teachers being observed to complete the information in the top box before the observation date. This form is intended for observers to acquire ideas that improve their own teaching. Recommended walkthrough visit time is 10–15 minutes. The form is best used with teachers early in the learning process about the Common Core State Standards.

Classroom Walkthrough Observation Form
Mathematics

Observation Date: _____ Grade Level/Subject: High School Algebra I

Conceptual Category: Numbers and Quantity   Domain: The Real Number System

Unit Title: Relationship Between Quantities and Reasoning with Equations

Standard Clusters: Reason quantitatively and use units to solve problems; interpret functions that arise in terms of a context

Mathematical Content Standard: Define appropriate quantities for the purpose of descriptive modeling

Mathematical Practice Standard: Make sense of problems and persevere in solving them

Observation Notes	Ideas and Questions
A pre-assessment was given where students were asked to perform two problems.	Good to ask students to identify consistencies that they noticed.
Students were asked to create a graph to visually demonstrate the relationship between two quantities.	See value in practicing and receiving feedback on concepts as a whole class before asking students to engage in independent practice.
Students received immediate feedback on how to build a function that models a relationship between two quantities. Students also were given opportunities to speak about their understanding of this function.	How does working with quantities and the relationships between them provide grounding for work with expressions, equations, and function?
Independent practice time was given after assessing student understanding.	

Interactions with Students (Notes)

When a student was asked to describe a problem in his own words about the relationship in quantities, he appeared to articulate a clear understanding of how to compare the properties of two functions.

NOTE: This form calls for the host teachers being observed to complete the information in the top box before the observation date. This form is intended for observers to acquire ideas to improve their own teaching. Recommended walkthrough visit time is 10–15 minutes. The form is best used with teachers early in the learning process about the Common Core State Standards.

Common Core Walkthrough Observation Form

Date: _____ Grade: _____

Subject Level: _____ Lesson Topic: _____

Common Core Content Standard:

_____

_____

Evidence in Learning Environment	Ideas for Own Teaching	Thoughts for Sharing
Evidence in Teacher Instruction/ Responses		
Evidence in Student Work/ Responses		

NOTE: It is recommended that this form be used by teachers familiar with the Common Core State Standards. This form enables the observer to acquire ideas to improve his or her own teaching and for discussion with teaching colleagues. Recommended walkthrough visit time is 10–15 minutes.

Common Core Walkthrough Observation Form

While in your class today, I noticed . . .

Thoughts and ideas I came away with for changes in my own teaching . . .

What I wondered about . . .

Observation Date: _____

Teacher: _____

Grade/Subject Level: _____

Activity/Lesson Observed: _____

Common Core Content Standard: _____

_____

_____

_____

NOTE: It is recommended that this form be used by teachers familiar with the Common Core State Standards. This form enables the observer to share feedback with the observed teacher and ask questions about the observation. Recommended walkthrough visit time is 10–15 minutes.

Common Core Walkthrough Observation Form

Classroom Walkthrough Date: _____   Grade: _____   Subject: _____

Lesson Focus: _____

Common Core Content Standard: _____ _____
_____
_____
_____
_____

Learning Environment	Student Work	Instructional Strategies	
		Modeling	Graphic organizers
		Guided Practice	Demonstration
		Active Reading	Reteaching
		Question Cues	Hands-on
		Learning Centers	Seat work
		Discussion	Cooperative learning
		Whole-class instruction	
		Small-group learning	
		Independent practice	
		Student presenting	
		Differentiated instruction	
		Independent practice	
		Other _____	
		_____	
		_____	
		_____	
		_____	
		_____	
		_____	
		_____	

	What are you learning?	What Common Core State Standards are you addressing?	How do you know if you are learning the material?	What can you do to improve?
Student				
Student				

NOTE: It is recommended that this form be used by teachers familiar with the Common Core State Standards. This form enables the observer to acquire ideas to improve his or her own teaching and for discussion with teaching colleagues. Recommended walkthrough visit time is 10–15 minutes.

APPENDIX H

Teacher Walkthrough in Action

Martin Luther King, Jr. Middle School is a grade 6–8 building in Beltsville, Maryland, housing 689 students and 54 full-time certified staff. The school is located in a suburban, middle-class, multicultural community. Enrollment demographics are 58 percent African American, 17 percent Hispanic, 11 percent Caucasian, 9 percent Asian, and 5 percent Other. The school ranks among the highest-performing schools in Prince George's County Public Schools.

During the 2006–2007 school year, the superintendent brought the classroom walkthrough initiative to the school district. He arranged for monthly visits by consultants from the Institute for Learning at the University of Pittsburgh who trained principals and staff members on the Principles of Learning and Learning Walk Routine. The Principles of Learning (POL) are condensed theoretical statements summarizing decades of learning research and are designed to help educators analyze the quality of instruction and opportunities for learning that they offer to students. The Learning Walk Routine, the Institute's signature tool, is an organized walk through a school's halls and classrooms using the POL to focus on the instructional core (i.e., how teachers teach, how students learn, and what gets taught to whom).

The Learning Walk Routine plays an important role in the continuing professional development cycle of a school or district. For example, if the teachers participated in professional development on differentiated instruction, time would be allotted for the implementation of that new initiative. Then a walk would be planned so that the teachers could observe the differentiation being used across the school. If the data from the walks show that differentiated instruction is not being fully implemented throughout the school, then future professional development will be indicated.

Under the leadership of the school principal, Robin Wiltison, the Learning Walk Routine has become part of the Martin Luther King, Jr. Middle School culture. The walks are an effective way to help faculty transfer and apply new professional development initiatives. They are designed to help the staff analyze the quality of instruction and opportunities for learning that they offer to students.

Over the course of the 2007–2008 school year, the staff participated in ongoing professional development on four Principles of Learning: Clear Expectations, Socialized Intelligence, Accountable Talk, and Academic Rigor. Staff members read and discussed articles supporting the POL. The walks during the following year were seen as an effective way to help faculty transfer and apply new initiatives learned from their professional development.

Each year, the focus of the Learning Walk was on specific areas for which the staff engaged in professional development. For example, in 2009–2010, the focus was on "clear expectations" as evidenced by observing feedback given to students, grouping strategies, and group management as they pertain to clear expectations. For the 2010–2011 school year, the focus was on differentiated instruction and multiple intelligences related to academic rigor for all students.

These walks are conducted quarterly, with dates established and placed on the calendar early in the school year. All staff members participate in the day-long walks. A lead teacher organizes the teams; prepares the schedule; acquires lesson objectives from teachers to be observed; records statements from the debriefing; and drafts a letter to the staff in regard to the purpose, findings, reflections, and next steps. Each teacher team visits approximately one or two classes, each for 10–15 minutes, followed by five minutes of "hall talk."

After the classroom visits, the walkers reconvene for a debriefing session. They review the evidence and questions raised during the hall talk. They look for patterns around the area of focus and the look-fors based on data gathered across the entire school. The principal gives feedback to the staff about the teaching and learning observed during the Learning Walk. The walks result in the identification of the next steps for follow-up professional development.

Third-Quarter Learning Walk

The focus of the 2011–2012 Learning Walks was academic rigor through higher-order thinking and questions. Professional development was provided by the Arts Integration and Socratic Seminars teams. The first- and second-quarter Learning Walk reflections indicated the need for professional development on student-led discussions. The Learning Walk look-fors for the third-quarter were higher-level questions (High Thinking Demand); arts integration through music, visual arts, and dance; and Socratic seminar discussions (Active Use of Knowledge). The principal sent an orientation letter to prepare the staff for the walks and look-fors (Attachment A).

All of the teachers conducted walks during their planning time on February 6, 2012. Before the walks, all of the teachers to be observed on that day were asked to share their lesson objectives for the day/class to be observed (Attachment B).

A lead teacher arranged a schedule of walking assignments (Attachment C). Each team consisted of three to four observers, and each team randomly assigned a group leader for keeping the team on schedule and facilitating the hall talk. Immediately before the walks were to begin, the teachers met to discuss the focus of the walks and review the behavior norms that govern the walks (Attachment D). Data collection forms were distributed to the teachers for them to record their observations. They took their observation notes using the protocol documents for the Principles of Learning from the Institute for Learning. Participants recorded only what they observed and did not make evaluative or judgmental statements.

Each team visited one classroom for about 15 minutes. Questions, which were developed by the lead teacher and based on earlier staff debriefings and Learning Walk goals for the quarter, were given to the teachers. The questions were designed to determine if the results of teacher professional development affected student learning. Students were asked the following questions:

- Can you name the different levels of questions? Do you know the differences among them?
- What lessons have you participated in that involved music, art, or dance in this class?
- Have you participated in a Socratic seminar?

Immediately after their classroom visit, each teacher group conducted a five-minute hall talk in which they discussed what was observed and what they wondered about, or questions they might ask the teacher to get a more detailed sense of the lesson. During hall talks, they organized their observations, compared and refined observations, separated observations from assumptions and conclusions, and crafted thought-provoking questions to discuss with individual teachers or the school as a whole.

The next day, the observing teams gathered for a debriefing session. The debrief had two purposes: (1) to analyze the observation data in order to inform the next steps of professional development needed by the staff; and (2) to help the principal plan for feedback to the staff in her letter. Each team recorded its observation data on chart paper as part of the debriefing. That debrief was followed by a sharing of data by all team walkers. The teams examined the data and searched for evidence of patterns of teaching and learning related to the focus. Then they crafted a series of reflective questions aimed at moving teachers to the next level of practice (Attachment E). Teachers used the data to plan professional development that would be assessed during the next Learning Walk.

Based on the feedback, Principal Wiltison prepared a letter to the faculty about observations from the walks. In the letter (Attachment F), she thanked the faculty for their participation in the walk and stated the focus and specific look-fors and the key observations and wonderings associated with the third-quarter Learning Walk.

The whole walkthrough process ended with plans for further professional development and Learning Walks—the professional cycle continues.

ATTACHMENT A

Learning Walk Orientation Letter

SCHOOL: Martin Luther King, Jr. Middle School   **DATE:** February 6, 2012

FOCUS OF LEARNING WALK: Features and Indicators of Academic Rigor

PROFESSIONAL DEVELOPMENT

Staff members were introduced to POL during the 2006–2007 school year. Over the course of the 2007–2008 school year, the staff participated in ongoing professional development opportunities on Clear Expectations, Socializing Intelligence, Accountable Talk, and Academic Rigor. Staff members read articles supporting IFL in addition to making regular "peer observations" with the purpose of recognizing IFL strategies and look-fors. During the 2008–2009 school year, the MLK staff continued participating in Learning Walks and the development of Next Steps. The 2009–2010 school year quarterly Learning Walks focused on giving effective feedback to your students, grouping strategies, and group management. Professional development for the 2010–2011 school year focused on differentiated instruction, multiple intelligences, and MSA strategies, including ESOL visuals; good-better-best BCRs in RELA; and reading stamina. The focus of the 2011–2012 Learning Walks has been on Academic Rigor through higher-order thinking and questions. Professional development has been provided by the Arts Integration and Socratic Seminars teams. The first- and second-quarter Learning Walk reflections indicated the need for professional development in regard to student-led discussions. The Learning Walk look-fors today are higher-order thinking strategies (HOTS), arts integration strategies, and Socratic seminars.

What could we reasonably expect to see in classrooms?

List one or two things that walkers should look for that would reflect changes in teacher practice as a result of the professional development described above.

- High-level questions
- Arts integration through music, visual arts, or dance
- Socratic seminar discussions

Which teachers' classroom will we visit?

Refer to the attached classroom visit and groups handouts.

Questions for students

What questions to students might demonstrate the impact of what teachers have learned from the professional development?

- Can you name the different levels of questions? Do you know the differences among them?
- What lessons have you participated in that involved music, art, or dance in this class?
- Have you participated in a Socratic seminar?

ATTACHMENT B

Third-Quarter Learning Walk Lesson Objectives*

February 6, 2012

Staff—Room 206A—Algebra 7: Objective, Activity: Students will work in groups in order to play a review game to analyze scale drawings. Outcome: Students will be able to use their proportions knowledge to solve problems involving scale.

Staff—Room 213—Science 7: Students will use multiple intelligence grouping in order to explain the importance of the skin.

Staff—Room 106C—AVID: Students will solve mathematical problems in groups in order to grasp basic math concepts so they can be prepared for future math assessments. Students will read and discuss "steps" to use in high school in order to be successful and graduate on time.

Staff—Room 104—Math 7: 1. TLW: Use their geometric tools in order to construct congruent line segments/angle bisectors. 2. TLW: Use the appropriate formula in order to determine the area of regions.

Staff—Room 209B—Science 8: Students will finish up Chapter 3, Section 5 on comets, asteroids, and meteors by visually reviewing the structure of a comet and discussing key points of asteroids and meteors; then in small groups review two exam questions that will be presented to the class and complete a "try this" activity locating micrometeorites in order to describe the characteristics of comets, identify where asteroids are found, and explain how meteoroids are formed.

Staff—Computer Lab/Room 203—Math: Activity: The students will work at a computer station in order to complete a Study Island Custom Assessment based on identified FAST 2 weakest indicators. Outcome: The students will learn strategies that will help them clear up misconceptions and avoid mistakes involving assessed objectives. Activity: The students will work in groups in order to complete a brief constructed-response question on measurement. Outcome: The students will learn how to determine a missing side measure when using the formula for area.

Staff—Room 102—Latin 1: Mod 1, we will be working with two different noun forms in order to translate a Latin story. In Intro to Latin, Mods 2, 3, and 4, students will work in pairs to match adjectives with nouns representing people and animals.

Staff—Room 109B—Social Studies 6: Students will identify how Earth's movement relates to the sun in order to explain seasons and latitude.

Staff—Room 214—Science 7: Students will describe the digestive processes that occur in the small intestine in order to determine how other digestive organs are involved.

Staff—Room 209A—Science 6: Students will keep an organized Science iNotebook; students will explain what causes mechanical waves; students will describe two types of waves and how they are represented; students will describe the basic properties of waves; students will explain how a wave's speed is related to its wavelength and frequency and calculate a wave's speed; students will complete characteristics of waves in lab group or with a partner.

Staff—Room 109A—Social Studies 6: Students will rotate through three stations to learn about the rotation of Earth; they will also organize their notebook and review homework.

Staff—Room 106B—RELA 6: Students will analyze the role of stage directions in a drama in order to determine how they advance the plot or add to conflict.

Staff—Room 202—RELA 7: *The Monsters Are Due on Maple Street* objectives: The students will analyze the action of individual scenes and acts and their relationship to the plot in order to respond to a BCR: discuss the plot of a drama.

Staff—Room 109C—Social Studies 8: Students will describe colonial America in order to compare and contrast colonial regions and analyze the impact of individual decisions and actions on society.

Staff—Room 114—RELA 8: Students will read narrative text in order to analyze the characterization in the text.

Staff—Room 210—RELA 8: Students will read a short story in order to analyze how a character changes through a story. Skill: Characterization.

Staff—Room 206B—Algebra: Students will use prior knowledge of graphing linear "EQUATIONS" in standard form in order to graph linear "INEQUALITES" in standard form and justify shading/no shading with two examples.

*Partial listing of third-quarter Learning Walk lesson objectives for illustration.

ATTACHMENT C

Martin Luther King, Jr. Middle School

Learning Walk—Third Quarter*

February 6, 2012 (Debrief February 7, 2012)

Each group should leave the last five minutes of its time for hall talk.

Team M6
11:00–11:20 a.m.

Group 1	Group 2	Group 3
AVID	Algebra 8	Science 8
Room 106C	Room 206B	Room 209B

Team L7
12:50–1:10 p.m.

Group 1	Group 2	Group 3
Introduction to Latin	Social Studies 8	RELA 8
Room 102	Room 109C	Room 201

Creative Arts
2:00–2:20 p.m.

Group 1	Group 2	Group 3
RELA 6	Social Studies 6	Math 7
Room 106B	Room 109A	Room 105

Team K
3:10–3:30 p.m.

Group 1	Group 2	Group 3
Science 7	Algebra 7	RELA 7
Room 113	Room 206A	Room 202

*Names of teachers within each group have been deleted from this sample schedule.

ATTACHMENT D

Learning Walk Norms

1. Walkers should refrain from making judgmental comments, whether disparaging or complimentary, about the school, principal, teachers, classrooms, or students.

2. Walkers should disrupt instruction as little as possible. If the teacher is engaged in direct instruction, then walkers must gauge how many individual discussions with students can occur without unduly disrupting the lesson.

3. When speaking to students, speak as quietly as possible.

4. If the walkers are not acquainted with the teachers in the building, then it is a good idea for them to wear name tags.

5. Walkers should respect the learning community of the school they are visiting. They should
   - stick to the agreed focus of the walk,
   - refrain from comparing the school they are visiting to other schools or commenting about other schools, and
   - refrain from using the Learning Walk as an opportunity to "teacher shop."

ATTACHMENT E

Third-Quarter Learning Walk

Debrief Responses

February 7, 2012

Evidence observed and patterns noticed:

- Lower-level questions asked.
- Students were held accountable for what was being worked on, with one student picked randomly to explain math problem.
- Students were working in small groups; groups by table answering questions to review for upcoming test; student representative from each group presenting each response.
- Students were working on a large whiteboard to display their answers.
- Teacher asking leading questions to promote discussion and encourage students to think and "dig deeper" (e.g., Who can help answer that? Possibly? Why? And again, why did you get that answer?).
- Review for quiz with students writing questions and other students answering them; students explained to teacher how they came up with their answers.
- PBIS strategy used—if answer was correct, they received a green circle to move to next question.
- Accountable talk in each group.
- Bump group getting help—when inquired about difference in group, was told that they performed high basic/low proficient and could be bumped up.
- Student work on wall demonstrates understanding of key concept; requires students to state what slope intercept means in context of problem.
- Puzzler of the week.
- Students explain how manipulatives demonstrate concept (graphing linear inequalities); a lot of manipulatives with students engaged.
- Peer assistance.
- Routines in place; students managed well.
- Students understood what they were doing and why they were doing it.
- Group leaders (students) in the center running and monitoring the discussion.
- Creating comic strips, songs, and writing descriptions of a trial.

Thought-provoking questions and wonderings:

- Why aren't they working in pairs?
- How are groups formed?
- How do we make sure every student understands, even when working in groups?
- How are visual learners supported? (Many directions are given orally.) Would the directions on the overhead and ditto help those who are ADHD, visual learners, and slow processors?
- Have you seen a difference in test results since using this strategy?
- How do you group students for test review? Have you used other similar grouping strategies for test review?
- How can we help our 6th graders move from activity to activity as smoothly as the 8th grade students we observed?
- How could this have been done with HOTS?
- Has the teacher taught the process for Socratic seminar? For Accountable Talk?
- On what basis were group leaders chosen?

- How do you ensure all students are on task?
- Is each student responsible for his/her own responses?

Feedback for future Learning Walks:

- A wall with HOT questions

ATTACHMENT F

"A Maryland School of Excellence"

Martin Luther King, Jr. Middle School

4545 Ammendale Road

Beltsville, Maryland 20705

www.pgcps.pg.k12.md.us/~mlkms

February 16, 2012

Dear MLK Staff,

Thank you for your participation in the Third-Quarter Learning Walk of the 2011–2012 school year. The focus of the Learning Walk was Academic Rigor in a Thinking Curriculum. Specific look-fors were: high-level questions (High Thinking Demand); arts integration through music, visual arts, and dance; and Socratic seminar discussions (Active Use of Knowledge). All have been topics of discussion throughout the year, and it was evident from the Learning Walk and debriefing that an increasing number of teachers have implemented related instructional strategies.

Staff reflection, during the debriefing session, was positive. It was evident that staff members enjoyed observing the activities in their colleagues' classrooms and that they were interested in replicating them with their students. While it was noted that an increasing number of teachers are engaging students in higher-order thinking (HOT) strategies, there remains a need to build capacity in framing HOT questions and making them part of daily instruction. The Learning Walk experience continues to strengthen collegial relationships and encourages interdisciplinary professional conversations. The following are key observations and wonderings associated with the Third-Quarter Learning Walk:

In every subject, students are regularly expected to raise questions, solve problems, think, and reason (High Thinking Demand):

- Teacher asking leading questions to promote discussion and encourage students to think and "dig deeper"
- Students analyzing the details in a novel, particularly the author's choice of words to develop characterization
- HOTS used in analysis, compare and contrast, and requiring evidence to prove response

Students in each subject are challenged to construct explanations and test their understanding of concepts by applying and discussing them (Active Use of Knowledge):

- Use of content-rich vocabulary
- Group leaders (students) in the center running and monitoring the discussion
- Creating comic strips, songs, and writing descriptions of a trial

Wonderings included:

- I wonder if it would help for students to have examples of HOT questions on the wall.
- I wonder how to prepare students for discussions/Socratic seminars.
- I wonder how to prepare students on how to answer questions.
- I wonder if answers will be discussed during class so students can explain/understand why a correct answer is the RIGHT answer.

The Third-Quarter Learning Walk provided the staff with an opportunity to observe their colleagues as they implemented instructional best practices. The debriefing feedback not only revealed areas of growth since the previous walks but also patterns where professional development will be helpful. The debriefing discussion indicated the following as possible next steps:

- Dedicate a wall to higher-order thinking questions or stems
- Professional development in regard to how to work effectively with small groups of students
- How to teach discussion techniques in order to prepare students for Socratic seminars

Thank you for opening your classrooms to your colleagues. I look forward to observing best practices as they are replicated in daily instruction. Your commitment to excellence in teaching is to be commended.

Sincerely,

Robin J. Wiltison

Principal

Source: Attachments A–F used with permission from Martin Luther King, Jr. Middle School, Beltsville, Maryland.

Appendix I

Evaluation of School/
District Walkthroughs

The purpose of this survey is to evaluate the school/district teacher classroom walkthrough process.

DIRECTIONS: Please circle your response to each of the questions below. Do not sign your name.

I have a very clear understanding of the . . .

1. **PURPOSE** for the teacher classroom walkthroughs.

   Totally agree   Somewhat agree   No opinion   Somewhat disagree   Totally disagree

2. **SPECIFIC FOCUS** for each of the teacher classroom walkthroughs.

   Totally agree   Somewhat agree   No opinion   Somewhat disagree   Totally disagree

3. **LOOK-FORS** for each of the teacher classroom walkthroughs.

   Totally agree   Somewhat agree   No opinion   Somewhat disagree   Totally disagree

I agree with . . .

1. The **FREQUENCY** with which the teacher classroom walkthroughs are conducted.

   Totally agree   Somewhat agree   No opinion   Somewhat disagree   Totally disagree

2. The **TIME** fellow teachers spend observing in my classroom during walkthroughs.

   Totally agree   Somewhat agree   No opinion   Somewhat disagree   Totally disagree

3. The observers' **TIMING** of various walkthroughs so that the beginning, middle, and closing of lessons are observed.

   Totally agree   Somewhat agree   No opinion   Somewhat disagree   Totally disagree

4. Observers taking the opportunity to **TALK WITH STUDENTS** about what they are learning.

    Totally agree   Somewhat agree   No opinion   Somewhat   Totally disagree
                                                           disagree

5. Observers **RECORDING DATA** about their observations while in my classroom.

    Totally agree   Somewhat agree   No opinion   Somewhat   Totally disagree
                                                           disagree

6. The means by which the observer **RECORDS DATA** about his or her observations while in my classroom.

    Totally agree   Somewhat agree   No opinion   Somewhat   Totally disagree
                                                           disagree

7. The way the **SHARING** of observation data is provided from those who observe during walkthroughs.

    Totally agree   Somewhat agree   No opinion   Somewhat   Totally disagree
                                                           disagree

8. Walkthroughs being unobtrusive and conducted in ways that **MINIMIZE** the interruptions to classroom instruction.

    Totally agree   Somewhat agree   No opinion   Somewhat   Totally disagree
                                                           disagree

9. My teaching and my students' learning having **BENEFITED** from teacher classroom walkthroughs.

    Totally agree   Somewhat agree   No opinion   Somewhat   Totally disagree
                                                           disagree

10. Classroom walkthroughs being **ANNOUNCED** in advance.

    Totally agree   Somewhat agree   No opinion   Somewhat   Totally disagree
                                                           disagree

11. The existence of a **TRUSTING RELATIONSHIP** between those who observe and those being observed.

    Totally agree   Somewhat agree   No opinion   Somewhat   Totally disagree
                                                           disagree

12. **ALL TEACHERS** being observed through the teacher classroom walkthroughs.

    Totally agree   Somewhat agree   No opinion   Somewhat   Totally disagree
                                                           disagree

13. The teacher classroom walkthroughs working well in **CONJUNCTION** with our other school improvement initiatives.

    Totally agree   Somewhat agree   No opinion   Somewhat   Totally disagree
                                                           disagree

References

Barth, R. S. (2002, May). The culture builder. *Educational Leadership, 59*(8), 6–11.

Barth, R. S. (2006). Improving relationships within the schoolhouse. *Educational Leadership, 63*(6), 9–13.

Bergmann, S., & Brough, J. A. (2007). *Lead me, I dare you! Managing resistance to school change.* Larchmont, NY: Eye on Education.

Blatt, B., Linsley, B., & Smith, L. (2005, January). Classroom walk-throughs their way. *UCLA SMP EdNews.*

Bloom, G. (2007, March/April). Classroom visitations done well. *Leadership, 36*(4), 40–42, 44–45.

City, E. A., Elmore, R. F., Fiarman, S. E., & Teitel, L. (2009). *Instructional rounds in education: A network approach to improving teaching and learning.* Cambridge, MA: Harvard Education Press.

Cronk, D., Inglis, L., Michailides, D., Michailides, M., Morris, D., & Petersen, N. (2008). Walking the talk: Instructional talk-throughs. *The ATA News, 43*(3), 1–3.

Danielson, C. (2006). *Teacher leadership that strengthens professional practice.* Alexandria, VA: ASCD.

David, J. L. (2007–08, December–January). What research says about classroom walk-throughs. *Educational Leadership, 65*(4), 81–82.

Deal, T. E., & Kennedy, A. A. (2000). *Corporate cultures: The rites and rituals of corporate life.* New York: Basic Books.

Dean, C. B., Hubbell, E. R., Pitler, H., & Stone, B. (2012). *Classroom instruction that works: Research-based strategies for increasing student achievement* (2nd ed.). Alexandria, VA: ASCD.

Downey, C. J., Steffy, B. E., Poston, W. K., Jr., & English, F. W. (2010). *Advancing the three-minute walk-through.* Thousand Oaks, CA: Corwin Press.

DuFour, R., DuFour, R., & Eaker, R. (2008). *Revisiting professional learning communities at work: New insights for improving schools.* Bloomington, IN: Solution Tree.

Elmore, R. F. (2007). *School reform from the inside out: Policy, practice, and performance.* Cambridge, MA: Harvard Education Press.

Hall, G. E., & Hord, S. M. (2001). *Implementing change: Patterns, principles, and potholes.* Needham Heights, MA: Allyn & Bacon.

Hord, S. M. (2004). *Learning together, leading together: Changing schools through professional learning communities.* Joint publication of Teachers College Press and National Staff Development Council.

Hord, S. M., & Sommers, W. A. (2008). *Leading professional learning communities: Voices from research and practice.* Joint publication of Corwin Press and the National Association of Secondary School Principals.

Kachur, D. S., Stout, J. A., & Edwards, C. L. (2010) *Classroom walkthroughs to improve teaching and learning.* Larchmont, NY: Eye on Education.

Lambert, L. (2002). A framework for shared leadership. *Educational Leadership, 59*(8), 37–40.

Lambert, L. (2003). *Leadership capacity for lasting school improvement.* Alexandria, VA: ASCD.

Linsley, B., Martinez-Miller, P., & Tambara, B. (2011, March 27). *Classroom walk-throughs: Linking observations of student learning to powerful teacher conversations about professional practice.* Presentation at the 2011 ASCD Annual Conference, San Francisco.

Martinez-Miller, P., & Cervone, L. (2008). *Breaking through to effective teaching: A walk-through protocol linking student practice and professional practice.* Lanham, MD: Rowman & Littlefield Education.

Marzano, R. J. (2007). *The art and science of teaching: A comprehensive framework for effective instruction.* Alexandria, VA: ASCD.

Marzano, R. J. (2011, February). Making the most of instructional rounds. *Educational Leadership, 68*(5), 80–81.

Marzano, R. J., Frontier, T., & Livingston, D. (2011). *Effective supervision: Supporting the art and science of teaching.* Alexandria, VA: ASCD.

Nelsen, J., & Cudeiro, A. (2009, December). Lasting impression: Targeted learning plan has a maximum impact on teacher practice. *Journal of Staff Development, 30*(5), 32–35.

Roy, P. (2007, April). Time to learn from and with each other. *The Learning Principal, 2*(7), 3.

Schlechty, P. (2005). Creating the capacity to support innovations: Occasional paper #2. Louisville, KY: Schlechty Center for Leadership in School Reform. Retrieved from http://www.mikemcmahon.info/capacity.pdf

Whitaker, T. (2002). *Dealing with difficult teachers* (2nd ed.). Larchmont, NY: Eye on Education.

Index

The letter *f* following a page number denotes a figure.

About the Authors

**Donald S. Kachur** is Professor Emeritus of Education from the Department of Curriculum and Instruction in the College of Education at Illinois State University, Normal, Illinois. He holds a doctorate in education from Indiana University in Bloomington. He served from 2001 to 2008 as the full-time Executive Director of the Illinois affiliate of ASCD.

Don is a workshop trainer for the Illinois Administrators Academy, the Illinois Principals Association, and the Illinois Association of School Administrators. In the business realm, he served as an executive consultant at State Farm Corporate and participated in the delivery of State Farm Advanced Management Seminars. In addition, Don served as a certified trainer with Motorola, Inc. for their Leadership Development Institutes for school superintendents and Executive Leadership Institutes for school principals. He coauthored the book *Classroom Walkthroughs to Improve Teaching and Learning* (2010). He has also published in the *NASSP Bulletin, Phi Delta Kappan, Kappa Delta Pi Record, Journal of Teacher Education, Journal of Staff Development, Florida Educational Leadership,* and *The Clearing House.* He is an active member of ASCD and served on its board of directors from 2007 to 2010. He can be reached at dskachu@ilstu.edu.

Judith A. Stout is a retired school district administrator and an independent consultant. Judy earned her B.A. at Mercer University in Macon, Georgia, and her M.Ed. and Ed.D. at the University of Oklahoma in Norman. She retired in 2005 with 19 years of educational experience in Lawton Public Schools in Lawton, Oklahoma, and nine years in Colorado school districts. In Oklahoma, Judy was an elementary classroom teacher, teacher of gifted/talented students, staff developer, elementary assistant principal, and elementary principal. After moving to Colorado, she was the Director of Elementary Education for Boulder Valley School District in Boulder for five years and the Director of Leadership in Adams County School District 14 in Commerce City for four years. She was on the team that developed the walkthrough model used in Adams 14. She coauthored the book *Classroom Walkthroughs to Improve Teaching and Learning* (2010). Judy has also published in *Educational Leadership, Florida Educational Leadership,* and the *Oklahoma Middle Level Education Journal,* and she has presented at numerous national professional meetings. She can be reached at jstout@lpbroadband.net.

Claudia L. Edwards is an independent educational consultant and the graduate coordinator for the School of Education and Behavioral Sciences at Cameron University in Lawton, Oklahoma. She earned her B.S. and M.Ed. at Cameron University. She is a retired classroom teacher with 29 years of teaching experience in the Oklahoma public school system. Her teaching experience ranges from kindergarten through college. As a secondary teacher, Claudia developed a transition program for middle school entry-level students. She also helped create a Saturday program for at-risk students and was the district co-trainer for cooperative learning. During her teaching career, she was a staff developer and an assessor for the National Board for Professional Teaching Standards, supervised entry-year teachers, and served as a mentor for student interns. She coauthored the book *Classroom Walkthroughs to Improve Teaching and Learning* (2010). She has also coauthored articles for *Educational Leadership, Florida Educational Leadership,* and the *Oklahoma Middle Level Education Association Journal* and has presented at numerous national professional conferences. She can be reached at cedwards@cameron.edu.

Related ASCD Resources

At the time of publication, the following ASCD resources were available (ASCD stock numbers appear in parentheses). For up-to-date information about ASCD resources, go to www.ascd.org. You can search the complete archives of *Educational Leadership* at http://www.ascd.org/el.

ASCD Edge

Exchange ideas and connect with other educators on the social networking site ASCD Edge™ at http://ascdedge.ascd.org/

Print Products

Assignments Matter: Making the Connections That Help Students Meet Standards by Eleanor Dougherty (#112048)

Classroom Instruction That Works: Research-Based Strategies for Increasing Student Achievement, 2nd Edition by Ceri B. Dean, Elizabeth Ross Hubbell, Howard Pitler, and Bj Stone (#111001)

Classroom Management That Works: Research-Based Strategies for Every Teacher by Robert J. Marzano, Jana S. Marzano, and Debra J. Pickering (#103027)

Creating Dynamic Schools Through Mentoring, Coaching, and Collaboration by Judy F. Carr, Nancy Herman, and Douglas E. Harris (#103021)

Enhancing Professional Practice: A Framework for Teaching, 2nd Edition by Charlotte Danielson (#106034)

The Formative Assessment Action Plan: Practical Steps to More Successful Teaching and Learning by Douglas Fisher and Nancy Frey (#111013)

How to Assess Higher-Order Thinking Skills in Your Classroom by Susan M. Brookhart (#109111)

Insights into Action: Successful School Leaders Share What Works by William Sterrett (#112009)

Taking Charge of Professional Development: A Practical Model for Your School by Joseph H. Semadini (#109029)

Transforming Schools: Creating a Culture of Continuous Improvement by Allison Zmuda, Robert Kuklis, and Everett Kline (#103112)

Where Great Teaching Begins: Planning for Student Thinking and Learning by Anne. R. Reeves (#111023)

The Whole Child Initiative helps schools and communities create learning environments that allow students to be healthy, safe, engaged, supported, and challenged. To learn more about other books and resources that relate to the whole child, visit www.wholechildeducation.org.

For more information: send e-mail to member@ascd.org; call 1-800-933-2723 or 703-578-9600, press 2; send a fax to 703-575-5400; or write to Information Services, ASCD, 1703 N. Beauregard St., Alexandria, VA 22311-1714 USA.